Praise for *Say Yes*

If anyone has been lying in darkness, may this book be your light turned on, your windows open and the light streaming in with every page. Scott has given us the hope and fresh air we all need after a year that has kicked us down time and time again. Scott Erickson is the hand pulling us up gently and kindly with every word. Scott, thank you for leaving the light on for all of us.

Arielle Estoria, poet, author, actor

We all must come to terms with how our lives have, and have not, turned out. *Say Yes* graciously illuminates how the death of a dream is not the end of our story but the preparation to the unexpected next chapter of it.

Jonathan Merritt, writer for *The Atlantic* and author of *Learning to Speak God from Scratch*

Say Yes is inspiring, but the kind that offers freedom, not fluff. If your life's purpose needs a metaphorical kick in the pants, this book will do it in the kindest way.

Kendra Adachi, *New York Times* bestselling author of *The Lazy Genius Way*

Scott Erickson comes alongside us with humor, grace, and wisdom to remind us that maybe we're not as stuck as we think we are. Through carefully crafted words and images, Scott speaks straight to the heart of things in a beautiful way I've never experienced before.

JJ Heller, singer/songwriter

Like a psychological roller coaster, with twists, hilarity, and existentially provoking content at every turn, *Say Yes* is an invitation into creativity itself. Scott Erickson's genius expression of self and community belonging makes a way for my own to come forth.

Dr. Hillary McBride, author of *The Wisdom of Your Body*

Almost no one likes to think about their mortality, and many live in the denial of death. Scott Erickson whistles us not past but into the graveyard and then buries us six feet under in belly laughs, tears, astonishment, song, wisdom, and true stories of human vulnerability that crush, surprise, and enlighten us. In the end, as we lie prone in our casket with Scott, a startling hope arrives as we surrender to our worst nightmares of abandonment: perhaps *resurrection* is the end of all things and not *death*?

Kenneth Tanner, pastor, Holy Redeemer, Rochester Hills, Michigan

Whenever my soul feels heavy and my heart needs encouragement, I run to Scott Erickson's art and words. From beginning to end, *Say Yes* contains healing and hope for weary travelers seeking to live lives full of love and light.

Nick Laparra, founder of *Let's Give a Damn*

Scott Erickson speaks with unparalleled creativity and transformational vulnerability to the universal question of how we are to keep living out a story we never imagined living. This message will help mend broken hearts and uplift weary heads toward the hope of dreaming new dreams together.

Jay and Katherine Wolf, authors of *Suffer Strong* and *Hope Heals*

Praise for *Say Yes: A Multimedia Performance*

Say Yes made me realize I had already lost my sense of wonder at such a young age. The experience caused flowers to bloom within me that I forgot had once been planted in my soul. I am grateful to still carry that bouquet with me today.

Trey

We had the privilege of seeing *Say Yes* in our hometown. We were so excited to see our friend Scott, but we had no idea the impact his creation would have on our lives. We were going through a major transition and that evening sparked a new fire that gave us the confidence and peace to move forward with our big decisions. We recommend *Say Yes* to anyone and everyone, young and old. It causes you to reflect, and it will inspire you and challenge you in the best of ways.

Veronica

I thought I was ready for *Say Yes*—as an Enneagram Type 7, my life is about saying yes! But what I realized through *Say Yes* is that I was saying yes to all the wrong things in life. I was saying yes to adventure, yes to fun, yes to what others wanted, but I struggled to say yes to myself. Now I have been launched into the journey of saying yes to myself, even when I feel like giving up.

Nich

I've seen *Say Yes* twice—once after a surprise breakup and once after a dear friend died by suicide. I left the first show reminded of how deeply beloved I am and encouraged toward wonder. I left the second show reminded of how deeply beloved we all are and reminded that life does get better after the crappiest moments. Both times I needed a laugh, a moment of reflection, and a kind word. *Say Yes* has delivered on all three, and it has marked my life for the better.

Rachel

I had no idea what to expect when a friend invited me to see Scott's show! *Say Yes* is a rare act of creative beauty and surprise. It was an adventure, and by the end of the night, I found myself on stage singing a duet with Scott surrounded by what felt like a room full of new friends.

Virginia

Say Yes is an invitation to not die—to not die emotionally, spiritually, and even physically. An invitation to contribute by just being me. To choose every day to be alive and not numb out, because my contribution matters.

Nancy

As a writer, I struggle with the self-doubt of my art and the average angst life can bring. I know I'm not alone in that. *Say Yes* felt like a dose of the antidote to the poison of discouragement that life can throw at us. I'm grateful for Scott's creativity and for inspiring the rest of us to continue pushing hope out into the world as well.

Tyler

My husband and I went to see *Say Yes* and were so deeply moved we bought tickets the following night to take our teenage son. The well-crafted story allows both humor and depth in a topic that is extremely difficult and yet so common. I still often think about how if we view ourselves "in progress," we give ourselves and those around us so much grace.

Meg

I'm married to the woman of my dreams because of *Say Yes*. I came to the event heartbroken from a recent breakup, but the show encouraged me not to give up on love. I flew home the next day and asked out my university crush. We had a quarantine wedding in April 2020.

Jared

I attended *Say Yes* at just the right time in my life. I was struggling so much with my worth as an artist, mother, and wife and had frequently considered giving up entirely. After hearing that the Voice of Giving Up says some form of the same thing to us all, I felt much less alone and was able to realize that I don't have to have it all together to bring value to my family or the world. I do that by just being here, by merely existing on this miraculous rotating planet, taking each step forward as it comes. I cried, I laughed and I experienced hope, and now "I'm on my way."

Ali

I was in my early forties when I saw *Say Yes*. Scott talked about Samuel L. Jackson acting in his forties. I had quit music when I moved to Nashville. Who was I to do music in this town? This show was one of a string of dots that connected something in my head. I'm forty-five now and just recorded my first song.

Kate

Something I've struggled with my entire life is feeling like I, and my environment, am devoid of meaning or significance. It seems like I'm always waiting for something big to make me feel alive, and my last few years as a stay-at-home mother of two little kids left me feeling like I really wasn't living in any sort of "special" purpose. When I attended *Say Yes*, I realized the thing that changed everything for me was this idea of cultivating wonder. Tapping into wonder is one of the most powerful and accessible practices for renewing my everyday life. I feel like I can trust myself again. I think I can feel okay about loving myself and staying in this full-of-wonder body that lives in this full-of-wonder habitat called earth.

Jessica

Scott Erickson curates an experience that reminds us that life is indeed worth living. While many of us have dabbled in thoughts of hopelessness, *Say Yes* ignites the humanity that has been dimmed by our world. There's no one I'd rather karaoke with than Scott, and there's no artist I'd rather lean into faith with than him.

Jillian

It was a wonderfully crafted show—we laughed, we cried, we sang "Escape" really loud in our car on the way home. But really, the images are what stuck with me—specifically, the image of the pitcher pouring water right beside the cup. I still haven't stopped thinking about that, and I saw the show years ago. It reminds me to lean into the love and grace that already exist.

Allison

Never have I been so delighted to be in a roomful of strangers imagining my own death. This show is so existentially significant that your life depends on it.

Hillary

I had faced the death of one of my biggest dreams and was still struggling to learn how to move on. Scott's liturgy gave me hope, not through repeating culture's narrative that it will all get better, but by affirming that it was okay to be mourning this dream I had lost and that it would take time. This was a major turning point in my journey to healing and discovering my new dream, and it has made all the difference.

Taylor

Say Yes helped me start dreaming my own dreams and gave me the courage to prioritize myself when the fear of failing others almost killed me. If you're asking the question "Why?," *Say Yes* is your answer.

Jess

Say Yes has stuck with me to this day. When I'm terrified to go into a new situation or put myself out there, I picture Scott the Painter dancing around without a care, like he did at the end of his liturgy of not giving up. I envision being back in that room, completely absorbed in the comical, yet freeing moment before heading into the reality of my day, hopeful that I, too, can implement his level of confidence into my unique human experience.

Natalie

SAY YES

SAY YES

DISCOVER the SURPRISING LIFE
BEYOND
the DEATH of a DREAM

with your guide...

SCOTT ERICKSON

ZONDERVAN
BOOKS

ZONDERVAN BOOKS

Say Yes
Copyright © 2022 by Scott Erickson

Requests for information should be addressed to:
Zondervan, *3900 Sparks Dr. SE, Grand Rapids, Michigan 49546*

Zondervan titles may be purchased in bulk for educational, business, fundraising, or sales promotional use. For information, please email SpecialMarkets@Zondervan.com.

ISBN 978-0-310-36193-0 (audio)

Library of Congress Cataloging-in-Publication Data

Names: Erickson, Scott (Artist), author.
Title: Say yes : discover the surprising life beyond the death of a dream / Scott Erickson.
Description: Grand Rapids : Zondervan, 2021. | Includes bibliographical references. |
    Summary: "Do you sometimes wonder what happened to the life you dreamed you'd
    have? Say Yes by storyteller and artist Scott Erickson is a profound, unique meditation
    on the three arguments of The Voice of Giving Up and the three mental health and
    spiritual practices that can help you fall in love with your life again"— Provided by
    publisher.
Identifiers: LCCN 2021029637 (print) | LCCN 2021029638 (ebook) | ISBN 9780310361909
    (hardcover) | ISBN 9780310361923 (ebook)
Subjects: LCSH: Spirituality. | Mental health—Study and teaching. | Self-help techniques.
Classification: LCC BL624 .E75 2021 (print) | LCC BL624 (ebook) | DDC 204/.35—dc23/
    eng/20211020
LC record available at https://lccn.loc.gov/2021029637
LC ebook record available at https://lccn.loc.gov/2021029638

Published in association with Punchline Agency LLC.

Cover design: Scott Erickson
Interior illustrations: Scott Erickson
Interior design: Denise Froehlich

Printed in the United States of America

21 22 23 24 25 26 /LSC/ 10 9 8 7 6 5 4 3 2 1

To the ones we've lost too early . . .
we miss your light.

Contents

An Introduction to Your Guide .1

1. The Death of a Dream 7
2. The Voice of Giving Up. .16
3. The Path of Desire 27

The First Argument

4. Nothing's Gonna Change. 41
5. Moments of Wonder. 50
6. You're on Your Way 58
7. The Light of Failure. 67
8. Bliss Is a Process. 70
9. DTR with the Divine 82

The Second Argument

10. You Suck and Are Ugly. 95
11. A Sacred Conversation. 103
12. You're a Contribution 109
13. Catalogue of Loves. 115
14. The Dance Circle of Life. 117
15. The Light of Worthiness .147

16. Dying Is Better Than Living 155
17. The Resurrection in Regret. 164
18. You're a Resurrection. 170
19. Death Practice 180
20. Not Giving Up on Yourself 184
21. Say Yes. 200

Acknowledgments. 206
About the Author. 209

An Introduction to Your Guide

Here we are.

I'm *here*. You're *here* . . .

. . . and what we know about being *here* is that life is a mixture of sacred moments while letting out a little fart at the same time.

Now you can't go to the comedy club and get too sacred because you'll be told, "Hey! This isn't a house for the holy! This isn't the place for that." And you can't go to the sacred space and be too crass because you'll be told, "Hey! Have some respect. This isn't the place for that." I think we all understand and respect the context for the sacred and the crass, their benefits and their limitations. But I'd like to submit that when we go to either one, we wish it were *a little bit more* open to bringing the opposite in, because we know that we are *a little bit more* than our carefully defined spaces allow us to be.

In order to have the conversation we really need, we need a space that's *a little bit more* of a mixture. My attempt in the pages before you is to create a space that allows your authentic, whole self to be a part of this conversation. That's what we're going to do *here*.

I say this because at one point in my life, I wanted to make a church service about suicide . . . *because I've never been to one.* I didn't know everything it would entail, but I knew it couldn't be bland and boring, like most sacred ceremonies are. You couldn't have a service on suicide that was so dull you felt like killing yourself by the end of it. That seemed very counterintuitive to what I was trying to accomplish.

I ended up creating a multimedia performance piece called *Say Yes: A Liturgy of Not Giving Up on Yourself* that is kind of a sacred/crass service about suicide. Well, not just suicide, but the spectrum of giving up that suicide finds itself in. More on that later in the book. Using the art of storytelling, comedic narrative, curated visuals, and crowd participation, I wanted to facilitate an authentic conversation about the universal experience of feeling like giving up on one's self. Even though it's not talked about often at the dinner table, I knew it was something every human being encounters; that in the miracle of life, at some moment everyone questions whether the miracle is a gift or a curse.

Suicide is obviously the most extreme way of giving up on one's self, but we also give up on parts of our lives in smaller and less obvious ways for a variety of reasons. Some of it is depression, sadness, trauma, and grief. Some of it is the existential dread that comes when losing a hopeful vision of the future. What I found in dealing with my conversations about giving up on myself was that I needed to develop mental health *and* spiritual practices to move through these hard conversations. I also found that those two kinds of practices are almost the same thing. You can have a great jogging routine to combat the depression that is darkening your days, but eventually on that run you'll bump against the question, "What is the purpose of existence anyway?" Our bodies and our souls are tied together, so naturally the ways in which we will embrace the gift of our existence will involve practices that deal with both.

I call the *Say Yes* show "a liturgy of not giving up on yourself" because *liturgy* means "the work of the people." Throughout the show, I involve three dozen participants from the audience who help make every performance one of a kind. Only by their contribution, whether through public speaking, singing, or being an intentional interruption, can the unique transformation to be found in the liturgy be attained. Every show is different because every audience's contribution is distinct.

I'm telling you this because it's your contribution that will make this book unique. I will be your story porter. I will carry the heavy bags of putting together words and images that hopefully won't lead to death by boredom. But the magic of this read will be finding your own story in these pages.

Which brings me to the elephant in the room, or the book, or the bookstore. This book's probable genre is Christian Spirituality, which is fine but admittedly isn't my choice. I'm very grateful for my partnership with Zondervan, and I'm overjoyed that they would pay me to publish a book with them. They've been a great teammate throughout the process. But if I had my druthers, I would categorize this book under something other than Christian Spirituality. Like Mystery, because something dies. Or Memoir, although it's a weird memoir with a dash of self-help, cartooning, midlife crisis, and a cherry of prayer poetry on top. Or how about *Life*. Can we have a section in the bookstore that just says, "How to Figure Out How to Do Life"?

This is a collection of images and words about how I've worked on living a life. All lives are unique but surprisingly relatable, and my hope is that telling my story will help illuminate part of your journey as well. "Christian" and "Spirituality" are pregnant with expectations, and I just want to state here that there are no expectations placed on you the reader to buy into any of these expectations. "Spirituality" just means we are going to have an honest, deep, and soulful conversation about life. "Christianity" is just the collection of sacred stories that I will be using to illuminate our present-day happenings, mostly because these stories are the most familiar to me.

The reason old stories are told in every faith tradition is that they aren't stories that just happened back then, but *they are stories that are happening right now.* I grew up in the Protestant tradition, so the sacred stories that help me with the framework of life come from this tradition. In no way am I trying to convince you of anything or urging you to sign up to become a member of my religious club. This isn't a cult recruitment manual. I'm just using the sacred stories from my tradition to illuminate how we are finding ourselves in the same places women and men have found themselves since the beginning of time.

Also, since I'm not attempting to sign you up for anything, my pronouns for God will vary from the commonly used pronouns one finds in certain religious circles. One writer in the Bible says God is Love, so I may just say "Love" in talking about the Divine. God is the creator of everything, the giver of existence, so throughout the book I simply call God "the Giver." Basically, any word you find in the middle of a sentence with a capital letter most likely will be a pronoun for God. Why am I doing this? For one, I'm an artist and I'm constantly dismantling assumptions to help awaken us to seeing the world differently. And two, I think creative play with language and imagery is just what you need from a guide on this journey.

Let me tell you what kind of *guide* I hope to be. There's a place close to where I grew up called "the Graveyard of the Pacific." Through the Pacific Northwest of the United States weaves the Columbia River, a 1,241-mile waterway that makes up a good portion of the border between Washington State and Oregon. This expansive river has been the expressway for salmon reproduction and human commerce for hundreds of years, leading ships from the Pacific Ocean to famous ports along the way, including the hipster capital of the Northwest, Portland, Oregon, and the birthplace of *The Goonies* movie, Astoria, Oregon. It's a busy waterway carrying more than $24 billion in goods each year, and a vital passageway for the surrounding area's economy.

Yet the river's mouth is known as one of the most dangerous waterways in the world—"the Graveyard of the Pacific." The strong flow of the river as it collides with powerful ocean waves has caused more than two hundred shipwrecks and has claimed thousands of lives since recordkeeping of ship movements started in 1792. Sailors must navigate rough waves, sometimes up to twenty-five feet high (oh, barf), while navigating the sediment-filled river mouth and the harsh wind and weather. Common mistakes by ships' captains can cost the lives of their crews and, over time, billions of dollars in an economy reliant on their shipments. Expert navigation here really is a matter of life and death.

That's where the Columbia River Bar Ship Pilots come into play. These specialized captains are brought aboard a ship specifically for this treacherous stretch of water. They don't care where you came from, what you're hauling, or even where you're going. They are there solely to be alongside the ship and crew to help them successfully navigate this tumultuous waterway. Their job is to be a guide through such a passage as this.

I'm not sure what you should do with your money. I'm not sure how you get perfect abs. I could offer some pointers on a good sex life, but I would end every piece of advice with a self-conscious "Don't blame me if it doesn't work out!" I'm not trying to become a self-help expert.

But I do know how to not give up on myself.

And when it comes to experiencing the death of a dream, friend, I've been there. It sucks, and it's a hard place to be.

I put this book together as a way to be a "don't give up on yourself ship pilot" who comes alongside you during this unsettling passage in the journey of your life. Your dream that died is most likely different from the one I went through that led to the contents of this book. That's okay. This book is less about what kind of dream died and more about what we do after this experience. I've been through this hard passageway before . . . and rather than offer pieces of advice on what to do, I want to invite you into a surprising way of living that comes only after the dream has died. I want to invite you into the mental health and spiritual practices I developed to move through difficult times, and I believe they can be invaluable to you as well. Along with sharing stories of solidarity that let you know you're not alone, I've worked hard to offer engaging imagery to help you find a new perspective on the unforeseen possibilities that lie before you. My superpower is to create a visual vocabulary for the spiritual journey we're all on, and my hope is that these images will replace the interior images that have begun to fail us. Everything from the words to the imagery is aimed at helping us navigate this crappy stretch of sea we may find ourselves in.

I'm happy to be alongside you *here*.

Let's begin.

Chapter 1

The Death of a Dream

What was your best moment of the last year?

And what was your worst moment of the last year?

Every January since graduating from the university I attended, I and my old college housemates and our spouses rent a cabin on the Olympic Peninsula of Washington State, where the *Twilight* series was filmed, and we spend a weekend together. We cook meals, wash dishes, play games, go on hikes, share our lives, and talk about anything and everything.

Saturday night dinner has become a bit of a tradition. While the meal is being prepared, we rearrange the furniture in the small cabin to make one long table. We all plate our food and sit at the long table together. Between bites, each of us shares our best and worst moments of the last year. This gives us a chance to be as honest and vulnerable as we want to be with our greatest triumphs and our most painful disappointments, which often are not the first things you bring up when you get together with old friends you haven't seen in a year. We've learned to create an honest space to talk about how we *really* are.

So let's do that here. I'll go first. I want to tell you about my worst moment of the year a few years ago that eventually led to the writing of this book, but to stay true to the tradition of the Saturday night dinner, I'll start with the opposite.

That particular year, my best moment was taking our young children to Disneyland for the first time . . . which sounds completely cliché, I know. But have you ever been to Disneyland with little kids? If you've only gone there *without* little children, you probably thought, *I don't know . . . there's just a lot of strollers everywhere*—and that's completely true. It *is* the Bangkok traffic jam of every stroller imaginable. But when you go with little kids, the experience truly is magical. Not only is it a constant fix of adrenaline and sugar brought to you by one of the best theme park designers of all time, but you get to see your children's wide-eyed wonder as they inhabit the imaginative world they've spent so much time only observing through a screen.

It's a real-life storybook where your kids get to meet all their friends they've spent so many hours with. Granted their "friends" are just hired actors in elaborate costumes, but they don't know the difference. It's their chance to meet their heroes—the women, men, children, and talking animals who have walked through complicated life situations and have come out on the other side with a skip in their step and a song in their heart. In fact, they even make a parade out of it.

Disneyland is the embodied proof to kids that the stories they have been listening to are *true*, like all great myth stories we retell again and again. So true, in fact, they even made a roller coaster out of it. It's such a fun and exhilarating time. I was depressed for two days coming off the high of it.

Now...what was my worst moment of the year?

Well, that particular year, my worst moment took place on a toilet. Now, it did not involve my bowels. But it did happen on a toilet.

At that time my wife and I were renting a quirky little house just outside of Portland, Oregon. One night, I put my kids to sleep in their bunk beds and closed the door to their room, and I noticed I was crying. Now me crying isn't especially troublesome. I'm completely comfortable being the bearded middle-aged man silently weeping in the theater during the Pixar film that suspiciously seems not to be written for children. I own being a crier. But I wasn't crying because my kids and I had just read a magical bedtime story. No, this was something different. I tried to stop myself from crying, but I couldn't. The sobs got deeper and deeper . . . and I made my way to the only bathroom in our whole house—a tiny little bathroom right off the kitchen—and I sat on the toilet and just wept. I wept for about an hour. Twenty minutes into crying, my wife found me and said, "Oh my gosh! Are you okay?" I tried to say something, but all I could answer with was more sobbing. She came into the bathroom and began to rub my back, asking, "Do you want to talk about it?"

"My tears are me talking about it," I stuttered. "I don't know what this is."

With the passage of some time and with some reflection on that moment, I realized what was happening: *a dream was dying in me*. For a long, long time, I'd had a certain dream, and somehow physiologically and psychologically my body understood this dream was never going to come to fruition ... and I was grieving the loss and death of it.

I'll go into detail about my dream a bit later. But before I do, let me ask you, *What is a dream?* How do you define it? Because we use the word *dream* to describe a lot of different things.

Definition of a Dream

A dream can be a series of images that bounce around in your head when you're asleep, a kind of mental processing of the day. Or you can have a *dream* house on a "street of *dreams*" or a *dream* job or a *dream* destination you'd love to visit one day. Or for a lot of us, a *dream* is simply the description we give to Ryan Gosling ... because that man *is* a dream.

If you were to look in the dictionary, which is a book about how we use words in our culture today, a dream is defined as *a cherished desire.*

Uh-oh. Did you catch that? I just used a sexy word. *Desire.* Desire is a frighteningly intimate word because it means *we want something.* I submit to you that what we want is not really the object, or the job, or the destination, but rather to be the *kind of person* who can get that object, get that job, get to that destination.

Maybe it's hard to think about it this way because in the Western world, "desire" has been commodified into a product pitch created by modern marketing. We've been told our desires point to something we lack, something physical we don't have, and our desires can only truly be satisfied by this new ultra-deluxe laundry soap, or that lavish cruise ship vacation, or this new and improved thirty-seventh version of the phone we already have in our pocket that is actually perfectly fine. The solution for desire has been put on the thing, and we know that the thing doesn't work, because two days after we get the soap, the cruise, the phone, we still feel the lack.

As a visual artist, I think about the images associated with the words we use to describe our world, our lives, our feelings. In thinking about dreams, our cherished desires, I pondered what we really want in those dream scenarios, and I drew three images I think speak to the *kind of person* we desire to be.

Tuning fork. A tuning fork is a steel instrument that, when struck, produces a constant tone that then becomes the standard to which all instruments are tuned. When we talk about our dreams, we are really talking about finding that attunement in our lives. Finding that chord where everything comes together in a beautiful harmony. *Finding the note of enjoyable existence.* Being comfortable in our own skin. Being aligned with our truest self. When we say we want to "have it all," we don't mean we want lots of stuff that is broken and in need of repair. We've seen that neighbor with seventeen broken-down cars in their yard. That's not "having it all." What we really mean is that we want everything we have to be symphonic, harmonious, and attuned to the true note of who we know ourselves to be. We want to be the kind of person who's tuned in.

Feeling suit. Imagine comfy coveralls or a snuggly onesie that feels better than the uncomfortable clothes we are wearing now. When we express our dreams, we are signaling that we hope there is a way to feel in the world that is different from the way we feel now. A dream job, home, or vacation is more about the better feeling you hope is there when you arrive at those things. To talk about a "dream life" is to inquire if it is better to be inside another life than the one we're in right now ... because the one we're in right now feels really complicated. All we really want is to love being inside the life we're living, like a super cozy sweatsuit you never want to take off. We want to be the kind of person who feels comfortable where we are.

Vehicle of destiny. To talk about our dreams is to believe we're headed somewhere. A car, or any vehicle for that matter, is intended to take us somewhere we desire to go. This desire implies we're on a journey. That we're not stagnant but moving. Maybe not always sure of where we're going, but we're moving toward some destination. We want to be the kind of person who has a destiny.

What was *your* worst moment in the last year?

I'm not going to pretend to know what it's like to be in your skin. I can't fathom the pain some of you have gone through. The losses you've experienced. The suffering you've had to endure. The disappointment you're still heartbroken over. Again, I don't know what it's like to be you. But my guess is that your worst moment of the year was something like a dream dying. The dream of the way you thought life was going to work out but it didn't. The dream of the kind of suffering you thought you were going to be insulated from and you weren't. The dream of the kind of person you thought you were going to become and you haven't.

If a dream is like a tuning fork, then the death of a dream sounds like everything in your existence is out of tune.

If a dream is like a cozy feeling suit, then the death of a dream feels like being bound in a burlap straitjacket of complicated feelings.

If a dream is like a car headed toward a destination, then the death of a dream is like watching that car burn on the side of the road in the middle of nowhere with no back-up plan.

If life is a miracle, why can the miracle hurt so bad?

I found myself crying on a toilet because I truly had gotten in touch with who I wanted to be in the world, the *kind of person* I had hoped to be by now, and I felt so far from being that person. I felt out of tune, clothed in uncomfortable feelings, and completely stuck. It wasn't that I was ungrateful for my life. On paper most things looked really good. But I wished I had known earlier in my career what I really wanted to do and then had spent the last twenty years doing that. I broke down because I felt like I had been missing a key ingredient in my life all these years, and now I had come to a dead end.

The Dream That Died

Do you know this feeling? Have you had a moment like this? Maybe without a toilet, but I'm guessing you have.

What was your dream that died?

Maybe it was to get into a certain vocational track.
Maybe it had to do with the person you fell in love with.
Maybe it was to enjoy the shape and form of your body.
Maybe it was to turn your passion into a career.
Maybe it was to maintain a hopeful outlook on life.
Maybe it was the dream of the family you hoped to create.
Maybe it was that thing you've been working on for years.
Maybe it was the commas in your bank account.
Maybe it was to have a more vibrant faith.
Maybe it was to believe more strongly in joy.
Maybe it was the song in you that wants to be sung.
Maybe it was to enjoy the gift of your existence.

Whatever your experience, I want you to know you're normal and you can find solidarity here. What a whirlwind life has been of late, and many factors we have no control over have affected and irrevocably changed our lives. But global circumstances aside, we all experience a death of some dream in our lives, because a dream is usually formed by seeing something in someone else and not being able to accomplish that.

Maybe you saw someone doing their thing and thought, *I want to be like them*, and you started to pursue that particular manifestation. You love music, and you saw Beyoncé perform and thought, *I want to be like Beyoncé*, and you began to work toward a career in music. Obviously, this is ridiculous. Nobody can be the next Queen Bey. Nobody. (Long live the Queen!) But we can believe that we should be like whomever we're looking at. The truth is that none of us can ever actually *become* someone else. Even if we acquired all the things they had, we still would never accomplish that dream, because we will never embody someone else's incarnation fully. We can only become the *fullest version of ourselves* . . . and honestly, none of us know what our unique manifestation of that looks like yet.

But we hope to know. And crying on that toilet, feeling the death of a dream, was the door of hope opening a little. I could now see more clearly my cherished desire. Eventually I stopped crying and spent some time thinking about what was happening to me. The question I found myself asking at the end of that time was this: *What am I going to do with this newfound discovery of the kind of person I want to be in the world?*

With much heartfelt discernment, my answer was, "I guess I need to start pursuing this . . ." And immediately after I uttered those words, I was confronted by the Voice of Giving Up.

Chapter 2

The Voice of Giving Up

What does the Voice of Giving Up sound like to you?

I want to preface the musings about the Voice of Giving Up with a little exercise on personifying our fears. Personifying my fears has become an invaluable activity for me over the last few years. Giving a voice, a presence, a personality to these ethereal voices in my head helps me get a handle on these inner influences.

Feelings and emotions are essential for a human life. They are part of our makeup as a species and are helpful in all kinds of ways, such as connecting us to flourishing relationships, alerting us to dangerous situations, or keeping us from eating truck-stop sushi that would most likely lead to relentless vomiting. Real best friend kind of stuff.

Often, though, we can find ourselves with certain feelings and emotions, and we're not clear on why they are there. An interior feeling or emotion that remains unnamed is like a ghost haunting our house. We don't know why it's there. It just roams around slamming doors and knocking our nice china to the floor while we huddle in bed under our blankets, wondering why we moved into this house in the first place. It's only when we confront the thing and find out its origin story that we're able to get control of the situation and exorcise the nettlesome spirit. This is every scary movie plot ever, by the way. Knowing why it's there is the mystery we're being invited to solve.

I found this kind of haunting spirit in my speaking career. I have been a high school teacher, a college professor, a spiritual preacher, and a performance artist. I've spoken at camps, assemblies, and conferences, as well as hundreds of times in one-man shows around the nation. In all those settings, I encountered the same fear that somewhere in the audience there may be a wickedly intelligent person, like a university professor, silently judging everything I had to say. This fear would always trip me up. I'd envision that at some moment in my talk, they would be obligated by their inner ethics to stand up and interrupt me.

"Excuse me. Excuse me, young man. I have a PhD in psychology, and a master's in theological studies, and I'm actually a relative of Leonardo da Vinci. So I know a thing or two about art. And I'm listening to you talk, and I know it's rude to stand and interrupt what you are saying, so my apologies to the audience, but I must inform you that you are wrong.

"None of what you are saying is actually true. And I think you should be ashamed of yourself for lying to this wonderful and kind audience.

"That is all."

That was my greatest fear in public speaking. That somebody smarter than me would call me out and I'd come to the revelation right there onstage: "You're right . . . and I think I should leave."

You can always tell a voice is fear when it asks you to leave instead of show up. Fear is a necessary emotion. It's there to keep you alive with helpful advice such as "Don't walk down that dark alley," or "Stay away from swimming holes with alligators," or my favorite, "Never ever ever guess if someone is pregnant." That last one will save your life one day. Fear is not helpful when it gives advice that seems to keep you safe but actually squelches your flourishing self. Fear's advice for public speaking sounds like "Don't get up and speak," "Stop walking to the microphone," and "Just leave now and go home to your bed and stay under those comfy covers forever."

Why did I have this fear? Some of it was dealing with imposter syndrome, the feeling that we're not qualified for the burden of responsibility we are holding because of our insecurities, inadequacies, and vulnerabilities. More to come on this later in the book. But when I reflected deeper, I realized this fear sparked from a moment when I was asked to speak at my childhood church as an adult.

I was teaching during the Sunday morning service to a roomful of adults I had grown up around. All very lovely, mind you. But there was one man in the back row who had "resting jerk face." He was also a religion professor at a local university, and from my vantage point, RJF seemed to dislike everything I had to say.

That moment proved to be more traumatic than I thought it was, because I kept carrying that anxious moment into all future speaking engagements. But after I discovered the root experience that formed that fear, I could begin to deal with the haunting.

Personifying the Voice of Giving Up

Since personifying our fears helps release us from the haunting of those fearful voices, I believe we should do that same thing with the Voice of Giving Up. And I would like to do so by recalling a scene from the second *Jurassic Park* movie: *The Lost World*.

I'm not talking about Chris Pratt and the updated 2015 version called *Jurassic World*. I'm talking about the original franchise *Jurassic Park*. I'm talking about Jeff Goldblum, Laura Dern, and Sam . . . Whatshisface. Written by Michael Crichton. Directed by Steven Spielberg. *Jurassic Park* changed our lives! We saw realistic dinosaurs on the big screen, and it filled us with childhood wonder. Also, Hollywood made about a billion dollars off the whole thing, so naturally they decided, "Let's do it again." So they made another movie . . . and it wasn't as good.

I wasn't there for the production meeting for *The Lost World: Jurassic Park*, but imagine that this was on the whiteboard during that meeting . . .

. . . while some movie producer was explaining, "We've had dinosaurs eating people on an island. Now we'd like to make a movie where dinosaurs are eating people in Southern California"—and that's pretty much what the movie is about. Steven Spielberg came back to direct *The Lost World*, and I think we all can admit he has given us many magical cinematic moments in our lifetime. But how he handles the problem of getting dinosaurs off an island and into Southern California is complete garbage . . . and we shouldn't let him get away with it.

But let's stay on track.

In the third act, a *Tyrannosaurus rex* gets to the San Diego harbor. It breaks free and begins roaming around the city at night. In one scene, the T-Rex is walking around a neighborhood, and it spots a backyard pool and proceeds to drink from it. A young boy is asleep and is awakened by the unfamiliar shaking thumps of distant Jurassic footsteps. As he sits up in bed, he sees this massive monster outside his window. The T-Rex stops, looks inside, and makes eye contact with the wide-eyed child . . .

And that scene right there . . . This is what the Voice of Giving Up is like.

You're lying in bed at night, thinking, *There's this thing I've always wanted to do. I'm tired of putting it off. I'm going to do it! That's right, I'm going to wake up early tomorrow morning and start on that dream.* And as that sentence leaves your heart of hearts, an overwhelming presence comes into your room, looks you in the eye—straight into your soul—and says, "Give up."

The Voice of Giving Up is like a wandering T-Rex standing outside your bedroom window ready to devour any dreams that may be trying to see the light of day.

So for the rest of this book, I'd like to refer to the Voice of Giving Up as the T-Rex of Giving Up.

The Three Arguments

Now, I've had looooooonnnnngggg conversations with the T-Rex of Giving Up. I've listened to its arguments, and they are surprisingly convincing. If I were to summarize, I would say the T-Rex of Giving Up has three consistent arguments it presents to me.

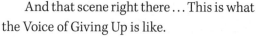

First, nothing's ever going to change. This miserable moment you're in, this miserable day you're having . . . Guess what? It's never going to change. The rest of your life is going to be this same miserable day over and over and over again. The thought of living in that is the worst. So why keep going? It's never going to change. This inner argument is the cause of most of my depression.

Number two: you suck and are ugly. It gets really personal for some reason. It's a real cheap shot for a large prehistoric reptile to knock you down and then kick you in the gut while you're on the ground. But what the T-Rex is saying is that you don't have what it takes to get to your destination of success. You're not good enough. You're not enough. In fact, there's something wrong with you, something you have no power to change, that will always keep you from getting to the success you want to have in your life.

Lastly, giving up is better than trying, or dying is better than living. And look, if we're going to talk about dying, we need to understand that dying comes on a spectrum.

There are lots of ways we can die. A myriad of ways we can give up.

spectrum of dying

I know you have the shows you like to watch, but you can binge-watch something every single night—not as curated entertainment, but as a way of ignoring the conversation with yourself that you know you need to have. I know you're just texting with your friends, but you can also tap your phone endlessly—not to connect with loved ones, but to prevent the fearful possibility of finding yourself alone with your own thoughts. I know you're a wine aficionado, but you can also open the bottle for another reason—not to enjoy its flavor, but to numb the pain that keeps calling your name day after day after day. There are countless ways we can give up on ourselves while we're still alive.

And yes, you can go all the way to the end of the spectrum, the ultimate death, and decide you just don't want to be here any longer.

The thing about this spectrum, and the thing about you the reader, is that you've probably gone through (or at least know someone who has gone through) some kind of death on this spectrum and come out on the other side. And because you've come through, you can tell us if there is any relief for us there in that dying.

For example, I have a friend who was addicted to video games. So much so that it was ruining his life. He played so much that it was causing his marriage to deteriorate. After one marital fight, his wife went to bed and he decided to let off some steam by playing video games for a little bit. "Just a little," he said. "I don't have a problem or anything." He played until he eventually glanced out the window to see the sun rising in the east. He had played all night long. He realized what he had done and was so horrified by his lack of control that he picked up his Xbox, walked out the front door, and threw it on the pavement. Then he jumped on it just for good measure until it lay in hundreds of irreparable pieces.

And then he got some help. Turns out he had all this childhood trauma that was coming up because of the intimacy of marriage, and video games seemed like a perfect way not to deal with that.

So my friend went through this death, this giving up on his life, and he came out on the other side with a bit of learned wisdom: "It's just distraction. There's nothing for you there."

You too may be someone who can tell us about what lies on the other side of one of these deaths, like numbing, distraction, or escapism. If it's worth it or not. If it's worth numbing the pain through substances or distraction, or if it doesn't do what we hoped it would do.

But this last one, this actual death—is there anyone who has gone through that and come back to tell us if it's worth it or not?

It seems like there wouldn't be anyone like that. But there are some of those people.

The Ultimate Giving Up

Since the creation of the Golden Gate Bridge, right around two thousand people have jumped off it to end their lives, and currently there are nineteen living survivors from an attempted suicidal jump. One of the survivors is Kevin Hines. Kevin believed he was a burden to those he loved. He was orphaned at a young age. He grew up in an abusive foster care situation. He had a lot of undiagnosed mental health issues. And in his young adulthood he made his way to the Golden Gate Bridge, hopeless and believing he had run out of options. He used his two hands to hurdle over the railing to the water below, thinking it would be a solution to his problems, but as he let go of the railing, he had an unforeseen experience that we'll come back to in a second.

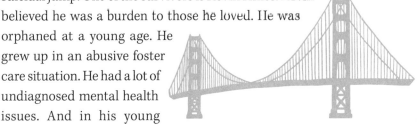

He fell twenty-five stories in four seconds and hit the frigid waters at seventy-five miles per hour. At that speed, water feels like concrete. But he didn't die. He broke a lot of bones, but he was still alive. And miraculously—I kid you not . . . this really happened—a sea lion swam up to him and kept poking Kevin's head above the water so he could breathe until the Coast Guard plucked him out of the water. What a miracle! The Coast Guard told him he was a miracle. They pull a lot of bodies out of the water every month, and almost no one survives this fall.

Kevin was in the hospital for a long time because of the

severity of his injuries. He had a lot of time to think about his life. When he had recovered enough to be discharged, he went around and asked the other survivors what they had experienced when they jumped, and they all said the same thing. In his words . . .

"The millisecond my hands left the railing, it was an instant regret."

Kevin said the moment his fingers left the railing, everything he thought was unchangeable suddenly seemed completely changeable. The only thing that wasn't changeable was the fact that he was falling toward the frigid sea.

"No one is going to know that I didn't want to die."

Today he is able to tell his story of what it's like to be on the other side of suicide. Despite how dark life can get and how alone it feels, there's no solution for us in taking our own life. Only a regrettable action that won't really solve what we hope to solve.

So as we look at someone who has gone through that ultimate death, we ask, "Can we make Kevin our friend?" Our friend who has gone all the way and come out on the other side. Our trusted friend who can confirm in us that the answer to our pain isn't suicide either.

But maybe Kevin's story isn't convincing enough. Kevin was walking a difficult road, so his suicide attempt makes sense, miraculous as it is. What's even more difficult to dismiss is when someone who seemingly has everything we want takes their own life.

This problem became most clear to me when I received the news that celebrity chef and travel show host Anthony Bourdain had taken his own life. I had been taking notes on my process of dealing with the Voice of Giving Up for a couple of years and was just starting to put it together for public discussion. The second time I ever shared these thoughts was at an arts conference in

Boise, Idaho. I had spoken that morning to a large gathering of artists and had spent the lunch hour receiving compliments about how poignant and applicable my content was to their journey. To share new work is a process, and it was a relief to know that my weird thoughts and practices were resonating with audiences. That afternoon I saw on social media that Anthony Bourdain had been discovered dead in his hotel room near Strasbourg, France.

The news devastated me. Not just because of the loss of a fellow human being, but because of the loss of what I viewed as a kind of career promised land. I'm not trying to be an accomplished celebrity chef, but I'm a similar creative artist, a maker, someone who creates and shares experiences. Anthony Bourdain was a seasoned maker, and he represented to a lot of us what we hoped our endless creative striving would bring about: that we could fully offer our unique talent at something while unabashedly remaining ourselves, and that our talent could even lead us to huge success, amazing travel, great adventures, and a celebrity lifestyle—and that everything the world has to offer would be open to us.

Look, I don't know what was going on inside this man. I did not know him personally, and to assume I know the whys and hows behind that ending decision would be absolute hubris. But for me, what it looked like on the outside was that even though Anthony Bourdain embodied all the success and accomplishment I hope for, for whatever reason, even he ultimately didn't want to be in his own life. If all of that didn't fulfill him, why should I expect that any of it would fulfill me? What could possibly fill the lack in me?

Each of us has some version of the T-Rex of Giving Up

whispering to us in our room at night that we should just give up on our most cherished desires. The arguments vary in their articulation, but they all have a similar theme: *you are the problem . . .* and in order to get to a life you desire, you'll need to get *you* out of the way. But we know from our friends, those we know closely and our new friend Kevin, that this is a lie. You are not the problem, and taking *you* out of the picture is the exact opposite of what needs to happen. "Life is a gift, that is why they call it the *present*. Cherish it always," says our friend Kevin, and I agree.[1] Your life is not in the way to where you want to be. Your life *is* the way.

But what are we to do when our dreams die?

Because to dream is to desire.

And to desire is to want. And to want is to want to be here.

And if you don't want to be here, then being here can be really, really . . . hard.

It can be incredibly hard.

---

1. Kevin Hines, "#TeamHopeNation," www.kevinhinesstory.com, italics added.

Chapter 3

The Path of Desire

Have you ever asked yourself, *Where does this desire come from?*

When life gets incredibly hard, this is often the place where religion steps in.

Now, there is no lack of theories and opinions about the positive and negative effects of religion, and for some of you reading this, a religious community has been a great gift to your life. For others, you're still healing from the wounds inflicted upon you in your religious upbringing. As a person who has both benefited from and been hurt by religion and the community around a particular religion, I have immense empathy for your complex situation.

I'd like to sidestep this conversation for a moment, because I know *religion* can be a triggering word for some. I'd like to offer a couple of definitions as we move forward. *Spirituality* is the process of making something invisible visible, and *religion* is the practices, rhythms, and rituals built around that visibility.

None of us can see our soul, but we know it's there. Our soul is that place in us that holds the depth of being alive. Whenever we come across something deeply true or meaningful, we call it *soulful* . . . implying that it points to the deepness of being. This is what spirituality is—giving attention to that which is soulful. We've all witnessed this aliveness in different moments in our lives. We've heard a song that lyrically and musically perfectly described what it feels like to be in our own skin. We've eaten a meal so good it made us tear up at the revelation that food can feed our body and our spirit at the same time. We've witnessed unbelievable, selfless acts of love that obliterated our most pessimistic thoughts about the potential of human beings.

All the innumerable soulful experiences in the world tend to have a consistency. Honest storytelling. Beautiful music, art, and the euphoria of group singing. Releasing of shame through confession and acceptance. Generosity and gift giving. Human unity found in a commitment to be together, no matter what. This is what every religion strives to be in its practices and rituals around soulful experiences. This is why all major religions share some similar practices—because from the beginning of human existence, these activities have always transformed us. We're transformed when we sing songs together. We're transformed when someone shares their story. We're transformed when we care for others.

But religion doesn't own the rights to these practices. They can also be found in recovery groups, book clubs, storytelling platforms, music festivals, and comedy clubs. Any human activity that is seeking the truth about a soulful human life has the elements we describe as religion. It's just that religion is very comfortable with the notion of God—the name we give the unfathomable, holy mystery we sense has created us but also feel alienated from. Just as is true with religion, many theories, opinions, and perspectives exist on who God is, what God is like, and what God is doing in the world.

My guess is that you have some thoughts about this. You may describe yourself as a member of a certain type of religion with a certain denominational perspective on the whole thing. You may describe yourself as a spiritual seeker trying to find the Truth in all aspects of life. You may describe yourself as an atheist, one who holds that there is no Force in the sky pulling all the strings, but you've found that life is this beautiful gift we are invited to show up for and enjoy for our brief existence on this earth. I get it, and as stated in the introduction, this is not a book that seeks to convince you of a certain religious perspective.

But God—the Divine, the Spirit, the Holy Mystery—is part of the discussion when we're dealing with the death of a dream. Because dealing with the death of our dream leads us to deeply existential questions about what life is and who we are.

When the comforts and securities of this life are removed, we are forced to witness our own weaknesses and limitations, and this vulnerable view compels us to seek others who can walk alongside us in our soul-searching journey. We may seek a coach, a pastor, a therapist, a spiritual director, a shaman, or just a wise community elder to help us navigate the darkened path we find ourselves on. Many of these wonderful companions are found in the faith traditions all over the world. Personally, I have benefited from the fellowship found in religious communities. We are made for relationships, and relationships that care for the soul are essential to a human life.

The Product Pitch Problem

All that said, the messaging about God that emerges from different religions can vary, as we all know. But much of the messaging about God that has emerged, particularly in our Western consumeristic society, offers the Divine as a solution to a problem. Maybe you've heard the advertising pitch before. It sounds something like ...

"Hey! I see you have this circle-shaped hole in your heart and you keep trying to fill it with the square peg of sex, drugs, rock 'n' roll, etc., and it doesn't fit, does it? No, it doesn't. Or you keep trying to fill that hole with the triangle-shaped peg of success, celebrity, and Instagram likes, but that doesn't fill it either. That's because the only thing that can fill that hole in your heart is the circle peg of God! And when you put God in your heart, you'll be made complete!"

And we make the Divine a product.

The problem with making something a product is if the product doesn't work in the way it was advertised to you, you get rid of it.

This toothpaste didn't whiten my teeth.

This weed killer didn't kill my weeds.

This God let my dreams die ...

And we walk away.

Another problem with making the Divine a product is it presupposes that the Giver of your existence hasn't been involved in your life already. If God is the Giver of all existence, do you think the Giver is unaware of what's going on with you? Do you think you have to get the Giver's attention, or could you instead pay more attention to the work the Giver is doing in your life already?

What if the Giver of your existence is the One who has led you to this place where the dream could die because *the dream was the thing standing in the way of a deeper conversation*?

The Discernment of Desire

This is Saint Ignatius of Loyola. He's dead now, but in the 1500s he was a young Spanish aristocrat who was salty with the ladies and had a talent with the sword. In 1521, in a battle with the French, he was doing his sword thing when *boom!* he was hit in the leg by a cannonball and severely injured. He spent the better part of a year in a hospital recovering, and he spent a lot of that time reading whatever he could get his hands on . . . which, at a time when hospitals didn't have robust libraries, consisted of the Holy Scriptures and biographies of the lives of the saints.

Reading these stories of people transformed by God had a transformational effect on him. So much so that when he had healed enough to be able to walk, he gathered his sword and military vestments, journeyed to the nearest Benedictine monastery, and laid them at the feet of the monks. He renounced his old ways as a warrior and dedicated the rest of his life to serving the work of God. He accomplished many things throughout his life. Most notably, he founded the order of the Jesuits, and he went on to develop many of what we now consider to be foundational spiritual practices.

Ignatius believed that one of the ways the Giver of our existence speaks most loudly in our lives is through our *desires*—that sexy, sexy word. But it takes discernment, because desires can either make or ruin our lives.

I believe most of us would admit we have a desire for wealth, but I also believe most of us would admit we haven't spent a lot of time discerning why that is and what we want to gain from wealth. We've all seen the desire for wealth lead a person to be generous and open, the greatest version of themselves. And we've also seen this same desire lead someone to be closed off and greedy, the worst version of themselves. How do we know which kind of person we would become in pursuing this desire? Discernment is essential because there will always be some kind of cost for pursuing our desires. Two people may desire one another physically, emotionally, sexually, and relationally, but they need to discern whether they will commit to the cost of what it will take to make that desired relationship work. We may desire a certain kind of vocation, but we need to discern whether we can commit to the cost of what it's going to take to learn the required skills to make that vocation a reality.

Our desires are powerful agents that can lead to our greatest flourishing or to our greatest destruction. That's why we're afraid of them. We're afraid of the covetous and lusty desires that spring forth in us at inappropriate times. Like the shoplifting desires at our favorite stores. It's frightening to have that energy in us when it's imploring us to commit petty crimes! But I don't think that's what scares us the most. What really terrifies us is recognizing our desire to have the same type of success relationally, physically, vocationally, financially, spiritually, even existentially we see in others. This desire reveals that we want to live a different life, and we're uncomfortable coming face-to-face with this revelation when we feel so far from that possibility. So close and yet so far. That's a terrible ache.

Deferred Desire

Because of this ache, it's easy to build an argument that we shouldn't have a life we desire. That it is somehow selfish, indulgent, or just plain evil to pursue a life we desire. There are various ways to come to this conclusion, but I have seen it most poignantly in the American Christian faith tradition I grew up in. Jesus said to his disciples that those who would truly be disciples "must deny themselves and take up their cross and follow me."[1]

And no doubt one of the core tenets of the Jesus way is selfless surrender in the name of love. But in an ancient-world culture, "take up your cross" had a lot of contextual meanings baked into it. The most obvious meaning is that people were still being killed by crucifixion then. Seeing a human being slowly dying on a cross was a common experience under Roman occupation. We don't live with crucifixions anymore. Crosses have become decorative and symbolic in our modern-day context. But without this hermeneutic consideration, two millennia later, people have concluded that Jesus is saying they should defer their deepest desires and replace that passion with a high level of church involvement.

Deferred desire can lead to all kinds of destruction through shaming, hypocrisy, and loathing. Shaming happens because when we've given up on our deepest desires for an imagined future payoff, we have submitted to an invented, quid pro quo scenario. We're following the prescribed cultural rules that require us to give up on what we want now so we get what we want later. Well, kind of. Usually in religious communities the deferment is giving up material stuff now for the payoff of invisible heavenly stuff later, which surprisingly can still reek of materialism. Are heavenly jewels in our heavenly crown really what we want? But

---

1. Mark 8:34.

when someone else breaks those rules and escapes the prescribed cultural norms, the secret dissatisfaction with the quid pro quo scenario we've allowed ourselves to be confined to is revealed . . . and our natural tendency to make ourselves feel better is to shame the other person. Which is where the hypocrisy lies. We want to follow our desires too! And yet we've concluded that we can't because of the fear of breaking social norms. Which leads to loathing. We may think, *How dare they follow their desires. How dare they succeed. How dare they not follow the religious rules like I do.* You can find other expressions of this loathing in the comments section of anything posted on the internet.

It isn't my goal here to spend oodles of time deeply exegeting sacred texts, so I'll let you get into that Jesus quote on your own time. I will say that in this very same Bible, King David in Psalm 37 writes, "Take delight in the Giver,[2] and he will give you the desires of your heart,"[3] intimating that the secret to finding our way in the world is more about cooperating with God than appeasing God. That the Giver of our life is also the Giver of our desires, which means that life has an invitational, co-creative nature to it.

What if the Giver of *this* desire is the one leading us down a path to bring that desire to fruition? What if the Giver wants the same thing for us that we hope for ourselves? Why do we always

---

2. YHWH, or LORD.
3. Psalm 37:4.

believe that the path of our deepest desire would be so far from the path God would have us walk? How is the path of desire so different from the path to the Giver of that desire? When we're living out of our heart's desire, we don't necessarily make that distinction anymore. There's no conflict between what we deeply want and what God wants.

The Vulnerable You

The conflict only comes in how we imagined it's supposed to look. This is why the Giver has no problem letting the dream die, because the dream is the thing that's in the way of having a deeper conversation about our lives.

What needed to die in your dream, your envisioned ideal, was *a version of you without vulnerabilities.* I bet cold, hard cash that in your dream, the you that was in there was someone without weaknesses. A version of you that is tough as nails, unwaveringly confident, knows everything, never makes a mistake, has no regrets, is able to do everything on your own, never has a moment of self-doubt, figured it all out early on, is the best of the best in your field.

Vulnerability is our relationship to our weaknesses, not our weaknesses themselves. It's the feeling we have when confronted with our imperfections. The image of being vulnerable is that of taking off our armor, making ourselves available to be intimate. To be touchable. To own our vulnerabilities is a move of trust. A move of solidarity. It means we have a weak point we can't defend against. Vulnerability is the act of making ourselves accessible and relatable. It is actually the true way to connect to each other, to the world, and even to the Maker of the world.

The deeper conversation about your life reveals that the only way to truly walk the path of desire is through your vulnerabilities.

This isn't a journey of you becoming the perfect version of yourself. That's what cults are built on. This is a journey about receiving the gift of yourself—the beautiful vulnerable you—and becoming a more wholehearted version of yourself wherever that path of desire leads you, whether vocationally, relationally, physically, or spiritually. That you're the kind of person who is relatable, touchable, and in solidarity with others on the journey of life.

When I was crying on that toilet, I was grieving the death of the way I wished my life—myself—had turned out. But after those tears dried, I was left with a choice about what I was going to do with this newly uncovered desire. Was I going to move forward in this risky and unknown new way, or was I going to just numb, distract, or hide myself away from the fear of showing up in a way I never had before?

And why was the T-Rex of Giving Up standing in my way? And why did I hear the same three specific arguments coming up over and over again?

Countering the Arguments

It became clear that these three arguments were the areas where I needed to put my focus. Not only did I need to develop counterarguments to the termination they were proposing, but it seemed that the arguments themselves pointed to a deeper conversation about the essence of existing, the nature of the Divine, and what we're supposed to do with this miracle we've been given.

Quite frankly, the counterarguments to the arguments are fairly simple. Just three simple statements in response to three T-Rex statements. But the larger conversation these arguments and counterarguments invite us to engage in deserves our consideration—namely, if life is a miracle, then why does the miracle really suck sometimes? And if God is the Giver of this miracle, then where is the Giver in the middle of all the suckiness?

For the remainder of this book, I'd like to guide you through the tumultuous passageway we find ourselves in after the death of a dream. I want to shine a light on the origin stories of these arguments and speak to why they can have such a devastating effect on our lives. I want to help illuminate the nature of their lies and offer mental health and spiritual practices to move forward on the journey I believe you're invited to take.

I also want to help you see that you're not over. That the only thing truly dying was an unhelpful version of yourself that was standing in the way of the gift of yourself that you're invited to receive.

Again, the three arguments we will be journeying through are:

1. Nothing's gonna change.
2. You suck and are ugly.
3. Dying is better than living. Or giving up is better than trying, if you want a little less intense argument.

The only prerequisite to taking this journey is bringing your present vulnerable self. If you've recently gone through any kind of a death of a dream, you're in the perfect place for us to make the journey together. I'm humbled and honored to be alongside you in this.

Ready? Here we go.

The First Argument

Chapter 4

Nothing's Gonna Change

Well, honey, these lions don't have manes because, uh, it's hot out and they, uh, shave the lions' manes to keep them cool in the summer."

This is the verbatim answer my wife overheard another mother say to her young son at the Portland Zoo when he inquired why the lions in the enclosure didn't have manes. My wife had taken our kids to the zoo on a hot Portland summer day and was gazing at the sleeping lions through the large floor-to-ceiling windows when this moment happened.

I just want to take this moment to address the fact that some of you reading this don't know if that statement is true or not. It sounds reasonable to shave an animal to keep them cool during a certain season, like they do with sheep or big, shaggy dogs. But, friends, this is not true of lions. Lions come from Africa. They live in the Serengeti. There's no way that evolutionary headscarf is preventing them from surviving a tepid Portland summer day.

My wife leaned over, mom to mom, and corrected gently and kindly so her kids could hear it too. "These lions are female. They don't grow manes."

Embarrassed, the mom replied, "Oh, thank you," and quickly

gathered her littles and moved on to the cheetah exhibit, where there was no chance of misreading a lack of manes.

When my wife told me this story, it gave me a chuckle, but then my laughter grew as I pondered this thought: *What if my wife hadn't been there?*

When was the last time your knowledge of lions' manes was tested before just a moment ago? In fact, has it ever been tested? This information from a trusted source—the little boy's mom, for goodness' sake—could have easily remained unchecked inside him throughout his childhood, into adolescence and his teen years, and well into his college years. I can imagine the embarrassing moment in his freshman Introduction to Zoology course when he publicly reveals this misinformation during the "Best Practices of American Zoos" presentation. My wife saved this young boy's future college social life!

Here's the thing. In our era of instant information, we can know a lot. Five thousand books are published every day. There's practically more written information in a *New York Times* Sunday newspaper than was ever recorded in the ancient world. We have the freaking World Wide Web. We can know so many things. We don't even realize how much we know already. We take for granted all the amazing things we know all the time.

I think that's why when we hear the argument "nothing's gonna change," we just assume it's true. We see it as just one of the many pieces of information we've acquired over time. We assume it's true because the voice sounds familiar.

When we are given information or told something by someone who doesn't feel familiar, we engage in a trust evaluation discernment process. We ask questions like, *Do I know this person? Can I trust their information? Can I corroborate what they're saying with other sources?* Just think of every time someone has come to your door offering you a pamphlet with the answers to all of life's questions. Either you were lonely and ripe for someone, anyone, to talk to, or you politely ended the conversation quickly because you internally concluded that people with the answers to life's deepest questions don't wear name tags and don't have the answers in a double-sided pamphlet printed from their home computer. We're pretty good at discerning a sham.

But when we hear something in a voice that has become familiar—even a voice from inside us—it's easy to assume it's true. We bypass all of our trust evaluation discernment processes. We would never tell ourselves lies, right?

But that assumption would be incorrect, because we've picked up all kinds of voices, statements, conclusions, and opinions throughout our lives, and they are telling us things all the time that can be way off. Like the idea that someone is shaving lions' manes on hot summer days in Portland, Oregon.

Unconscious Narratives

The famous psychotherapist Carl Jung said, **"Until you make the unconscious conscious, it will direct your life and you will call it fate."**[1]

We are narrative-making machines. Our five senses are taking in way more information than we could ever possibly know or understand. Our senses gather all this information and synthesize it into a simple narrative. And mostly it sounds like, *Am I safe or not in this situation?*

---

1. Quoted in Neel Burton, "Jung: The Man and His Symbols," *Psychology Today*, April 8, 2012, www.psychologytoday.com/us/blog/hide-and-seek/201204/jung -the-man-and-his-symbols.

Wherever you are reading this book—in a coffee shop, at your house, on a bus or an airplane—when you entered that place, your senses examined everything around you and in a split second developed a narrative of whether you were safe or not. You probably weren't even aware of the process, but it happened. That's why you're comfortably sitting and reading this book. If you had walked into this space and noticed a pack of wild wolves lingering hungrily in the corner, you would have hightailed it out of there, saying to yourself, *I wasn't planning to get eaten alive today.* This safety discernment is happening all the time, whether you're aware of it or not. And thank God, because who knows how many rooms with wild wolves we would've stayed in if the discernment filter hadn't been on.

Safety narratives are the predominant narrative we encounter every day. From where to park our car in a parking garage, to what food to order at a new restaurant, to what kind of beliefs we should or shouldn't have in the religious culture we're in. Oh yes. Safety through belonging is a massive influence on the beliefs we hold on to when we're part of a communal faith. We'll hit on that in a moment.

But we also have narratives that sound something like this:

This is who I am.
This is what I'm capable of doing.
This is where my life is headed.

These narratives are a bit more insidious because they were formed in us by the way our parents talked to us as kids, the way adults treated us when we were young, and the way we learned to survive in the world as vulnerable children. And just like our safety narratives, these are working all the time too.

Author and family expert Peggy O'Mara puts it this way: "The way you talk to your child becomes his or her inner voice."[2] That quote freaks me out as a parent because I know it's true. I do wonder what my kids will discuss with their therapist about me one day. I imagine it going like, "My dad is an artist. I know he loves me, but he spent an awful amount of time staring into the nothing, slowly nodding his head."

I'm also the child of parents who taught me an internal voice, just as you are, however that went for you. And no matter how our parents were (mine were great), nobody escapes internalizing the things they said about life, themselves, beliefs, politics, our futures, and the possibilities. All these ideas implanted themselves in us in ways we will be unpacking our whole lives.

Even if you have great parents like I do, we've all adopted twisted narratives regardless. And abuse leads to all kinds of destructive internal narratives about one's worth and safety in the world. Many of my friends endured some kind of abuse when they were kids, and as adults they're still living with the hauntings of those experiences. I was sexually abused by a babysitter when I was in elementary school, and now as an adult, a much-needed date night with my wife comes with much anxiety as I question whether my kids are safe with the person watching them.

PAST

Your narrative is the story you believe you are living in. It is the constructed account of what happened and therefore what most likely *will* happen based on your previous information.

We really don't see anything as it is now. We only see now

2. Peggy O'Mara, "The Voices of Mothers Matter," peggyomara.com, January 6, 2020, www.peggyomara.com/2020/01/06/the-voices-of-mothers/#genesis-content.

through the lens of the past. All this information is creating an embodied narrative we live out every day, because the words that have been said and the actions that have been experienced live in our body.

Formative Narratives

We can remember the good and the bad actions that have been done to our body. Some left physical scars, like skateboard jumps gone wrong or that time we learned on a family camping trip that pocketknives are really sharp. Others are harder to see but they're there, like a hug from a romantic crush or that decades-old fracture or the physical memory of our first car crash.

But words live in our bodies too. Like that time someone called you stupid. Or clumsy. Or told you your butt was too big. Or you're just always in the way. These words are stating a conclusion about you, a narrative about the story you're in, and at a vulnerable and formative time—especially out of the mouth of a trusted adult—these words can become the framing narrative we believe all the way into our adulthood.

Formative narratives don't just come from one adult, but they develop in communal settings as well. Microcommunities—a small town, summer camp, or hobby-based group such as the Girl Scouts of America—can have shared values and perspectives that are massively formative for children who grow up in them. This is especially true in any kind of religious community. In addition to meeting our deep need for communal belonging, religion also offers an explanation for how the universe works, who we are— good or bad, loved or unlovable—what we should be ashamed of, who the enemy is, even where we are headed and how we get on the good side. Basically, as kids we were taught lessons on how to live if we want to succeed in the world. Not necessarily in a job, although there are plenty of thoughts on that too, but how to maintain safety.

Religion teaches us how to find safety through belonging. Usually it means saying we believe in a set of core beliefs, and as long as we don't question or deny any of those, we're in! But those parameters, those rules of belonging, are tenuous. If we get divorced, we're out. If we stop believing in a certain thing, we're out. If we have questions that are so threatening they seem like they might take down the entire system, we're out. And so on and so forth.

We call our childhood our "formative years" because those years play a huge part in how we strategize to succeed for the rest of our lives. How we are formed to think about existence. How we are formed to communicate with others. How we are formed to see the world—and *how we see the world* is rarely the same thing as *how the world actually is.*

Destructive Narratives

At the point of my breakdown, I had some really bad narratives. I've always danced with depression and periodic sadness. Some of it may be my physical makeup and personality type. I'm an Enneagram 4, if you know what that means, and often it seems like my kindred spirit is Eeyore from the Winnie the Pooh universe. I'm a personality that feels a lot, and some days there are a lot of low feelings.

But the internal narratives framing the way I saw everything were playing into this too. Especially around the time of the toilet incident when I was dealing with the sadness of wishing my life had turned out a different way. Along with those emotions came some very destructive narratives about my life and myself. Narratives like:

I'm supposed to be walking down another path ...
I'm supposed to be a better kind of person than I am now ...
I should be way more successful than I am ...
I'm stuck in this early childhood parental nightmare of lack
of sleep, lack of help, nonstop dishes, and a soul-crushing
amount of laundry, and I'm never going to get out of it ...
I'm almost forty and my life isn't turning out how I hoped ...

There's no way to change the past. There's no time machine. No genie in a bottle to grant my wishes. The death of a dream is the consequence of my past choices, and now I'm left with the regret, the ghosts of what "should've" been. I should've walked

down another path. I should've made different choices. I should've ended up somewhere different.

For me, my most depressive time is when I listen to the narrative of "nothing's gonna change," because in some ways it's true.

Nothing *is* going to change ... in the past. I am where I am, and I can't change how I got here. But then the T-Rex makes a sly argument that this miserable moment *is* reality, and this *is* the way I'm going to feel for the rest of my life. It predicts that this low moment, this dead end to my dreams, is the final destination, and I blew it. I drove all this way to end up at a dead end.

"Nothing's gonna change" is a safety narrative. It offers numbing, distraction, and giving up as ways to deal with this failure. There's safety in believing this lie, deflecting counternarratives, defending our belief, and isolating ourselves from others because doing so allows us the ability to make sense of our past. It allows us familiarity and comfort regarding why we have arrived where we are at.

But "nothing's gonna change" overlooks two things. One, nothing *is* gonna change the past, but how I look at the past *can* change. And two, maybe this low point is a necessary moment that will launch me into the change I've always wanted.

Around the time of my breakdown, I was working with a therapist who encouraged me to pay attention to what I was saying to myself. I needed to listen to my self-talk and write it down in a journal so I could see what I was saying to myself. So I did.

But as I was capturing all of these narratives, I wondered if there was ever a time when I didn't have narratives. I'm not sure if we're ever without narratives, but I wondered if there could ever be moments when I would be so enraptured by what was happening that the narratives, and everything I think I know, were just put on hold for a while. Are there ever moments like these?

It turns out there are . . . and we call them *moments of wonder.*

Chapter 5

Moments of Wonder

Have you ever been to a concert?

The elements of every concert consist of similar things: some musicians, some instruments, some lights, a sound system, a venue, an audience . . . and all of these elements work together to create an experience.

But every concert has a moment when the individual elements seemingly transcend their individuality to coalesce into something larger. It becomes wonderful, grandiose, hypnotic, all-encompassing, and you're there witnessing it, jumping up and down in a field with thousands of other fans, screaming out, "I don't know what's happening, but I'm glad I'm here!" And you are! You don't want to be anywhere else. You're just right there in that wondrous moment.

Or I surf. Sometimes. I mean, I live in Austin, Texas, which lacks oceanfront property. But I grew up surfing in the Pacific Northwest, which lacks any kind of warmth. Wonder can happen pretty much anywhere, but surfing has a unique partnership with wonder. First, the surface you're on is literally moving up and down, in and out, and you can dive underneath it or balance on top of it. It's alive. Animals are living below and above that surface. Weather patterns are unfolding at the meeting of the sea and the land. The tides are affected by an orbiting moon hundreds of thousands of miles away. You mostly miss all this because your attention is focused on not drowning as you paddle out through the unrelenting breakers. But there is always a moment, if you're paying attention, after you make it through the breakers and sit up on your board to catch your breath, when you'll see all this intertwined glory unfolding around you, and you'll be overwhelmed by the immensity of it all and be filled with wonder.

My wife and I met and were married in Seattle, Washington, and we lived there for the first four years of our marriage. Then I was offered an artist-in-residence job in Houston, Texas, and when you're an artist and someone wants to pay you to make art, you take that job. We packed all our material possessions in a moving truck and decided to make our trek from Seattle to Houston a bit of a sightseeing tour of the western United States.

The first place we stopped was called Craters of the Moon National Monument in Idaho. I had never heard of this national monument, but apparently thousands of years ago, before the land was ever called Idaho, a volcano exploded and blanketed the landscape with rock and lava. It has since cooled and hardened, and with the lack of vegetation, the area resembles the surface of the moon. In fact, it's so moonlike that even the Apollo missions astronauts trained there to learn field geology and log some hours in their moon buggies.

Another fun fact about Craters of the Moon: it's one of the least light-polluted places in the United States. We planned on tent camping there, and when we checked into our campsite, the ranger recommended we stay up late to see the stars. "The stars are amazing here! You need to stay up late." And we were like, "We will!" We set up camp and shared a bottle of wine after dinner to pass the time, and at midnight we were zonked. The stars were cool. But not *that* cool. So we went to bed.

At four in the morning, my wife nudged me, communicating her need to pee. I needed to too, so I suggested we walk to the toilets together in the dark. And when we stepped out of the tent, we looked up.

Wha—!

This!

So many stars! More than I knew existed!

Having spent my whole life in cities where the standard sixteen stars are out every night, I had no idea what the night sky really looks like when there is no light pollution. And I was filled with wonder. And pee. I mean, we were stumbling along, looking at the sky in the dark as we made our way to the bathroom. I was going to explode if I didn't! But afterward we gazed at the infinite canopy, taking in the cosmic beauty of it all, filled with wonder.

Wonder Filters

Renowned professor and mythologist Joseph Campbell said, "People say that what we're all seeking is a meaning for life. I don't think that's what we're really seeking. I think that what we're seeking is an experience of *being alive*, so that our life experiences on the purely physical plane will have resonances with our own innermost being and reality, so that we actually feel the rapture of being alive."[1]

I think he's on to something there. To pursue the answer to the question of the meaning of life is to pursue knowledge. But the pursuit of wonder is our attempt to experience being alive.

Wonder is the rapturous experience of being alive.

It's that moment when all our narratives about what is happening grow delightfully silent and we're able, even for just a moment, to see reality for the beautiful gift it is.

Try to recall the last time you experienced wonder. Was it in nature? Rounding the last bend on your climb to a mountain peak, seeing a view that took your breath away? Or was it the last time you laughed so hard you began to cry? Or when you were caught off guard by beautiful street art found in a dingy alley? Or when you tasted something so good it made you emotional?

What's the common denominator in all these experiences? What's the connection between stars, food, laughter, surfing, the ocean, the concert?

The common denominator is you.

Wonder is not an exterior destination to arrive at, like a mountaintop view or a once-in-a-lifetime concert. Those experiences may bring that feeling. But *wonder is an internal filter through which we learn to look at life.*

This filter is always there, but it is most easily accessible to us in new situations—when we don't have a narrative about what's happening yet. If we want to feel the rapturous experience of

---

1. Joseph Campbell with Bill Moyers, *The Power of Myth* (New York: Anchor, 1991), 4–5, emphasis added.

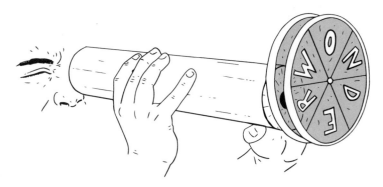

being alive more often, then removing the filter of familiarity is the practice we most need to adopt.

For example, if you've ever traveled to a new city, you probably remember being awed by the beautiful architecture or the exotic sights and sounds all around you, thinking, *This place is amazing!* Then three days later you said, "Let's get out of here. I'm so bored!" What happened? Did the place change? No, you did. You got familiar with everything, and familiarity kills wonder.

Familiarity Kills Wonder

Of course, familiarity is also a helpful tool. In a new situation our senses are working overtime to take in everything before us. We are often calculating whether we're safe or not. Familiarity is the adaptive narrative that catalogues the "new things" into the "known things" file. The unsafe to the safe. Familiarity allows our senses to take a much-needed break from saving our lives constantly.

Familiarity helps when your kids and their friends are having a sleepover in your living room but you need to get some water from the kitchen in the middle of the night and you've gotta navigate the dark room from memory without stubbing your toe. Or driving home lost in thought and arriving safely without really remembering the process of getting there. Or successfully picking up in-line skating again after fifteen years of being "off the blade." Or so I've heard . . .

But familiarity becomes unhelpful when you've been married a long time and you find yourself bored with your spouse. I mean, I've only heard about this from a friend, but it makes sense. You think you know everything about them, and there's nothing new anymore. Or when you show up to your job every day in your same body with the same people around. You begin to repeat the narrative, *Everything is the same. Nothing changes. I can't really change my situation. Nothing's gonna change.* Familiarity kills wonder and stands in the way of the ever-evolving future.

In Johann Hari's fantastic book *Lost Connections*, he describes nine major causes of depression and anxiety, all of which are a disconnection from something that enables human flourishing.[2] One of those nine is a disconnection from a hopeful or secure future. A future you can see yourself in. A future you can look forward to. A future that gives you hope to make it through the darkest of times. The T-Rex of Giving Up is standing in the way of that vision. It's saying there is no future like that for you. All you have is now, this miserable moment. And as far as it's concerned, you should just expect this for the rest of your life.

I can't do anything about this pain.

This is as smart as I can get.

I hate this job, but it's the only thing I'm good at.

These narratives stick around because they are familiar. They are comforting, like a kind of Stockholm syndrome,[3] because at least we know them and what it takes to survive them. Not thrive,

---

2. See Johann Hari, *Lost Connections: Uncovering the Real Causes of Depression—and the Unexpected Solutions* (New York: Bloomsbury, 2018).
3. A psychological response that can occur when hostages or abuse victims bond with their captors or abusers.

but survive. But, beloved, you're not reading this book to merely survive. You're taking the steps to live in a way that thrives. To change your narratives, to grow, to attempt something new is to become uncomfortable. To become *unnarrativeable*. Not a word, I know, but roll with my bad English for a second. You must leave what you know—at least the narrative of what you know—to launch into the frightening but hopeful potential of what is unknown.

Accessing Wonder

This is where wonder can help us change our narratives. When we pause our narratives for a bit, we see that our narratives *can* be paused. Meaning, they're not the framework of reality but a story we are bringing to interpret reality. And when we see that, we can choose an alternative story, one that will help us move forward in pursuing our deepest desire.

So we should go to concerts and look at the stars and swim in the ocean because those things revive the wonder in us, the rapturous experience of being alive. But we also have jobs, children, and responsibilities, and we can't do those things every day. Unless we're trust fund kids. Then we just swim in the ocean, go to concerts, and look at the stars every day, probably on the French Riviera. I assume that's what trust fund kids do with their time. But even then, I imagine looking at the stars every night from your humongous yacht loses its wonder after a while.

I started asking myself if there was a way I could hack the wonder filter on a daily basis. Was there a simple way to view reality without a familiar narrative and with more of an inviting possibility?

I began by examining the ingredients of wonder, and soon I found a simple practice that allowed me to experience daily moments of wonder without having to climb a mountain peak every day. And so far it works! I've been developing it for years now. But before I share it with you, I want you to look at some art to experience what happens in you in a moment of wonder.

Chapter 6

You're on Your Way

Artist Scott Listfield has a series of delightful paintings in which he portrays an astronaut walking around our world void of any people.[1] This vacant world could be a postapocalyptic world, but nothing is really destroyed. It's just empty of people, and thus empty of a narrative.

art school breakdown

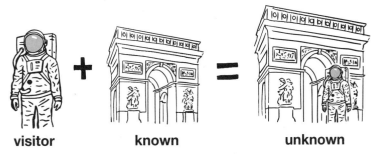

visitor + **known** = **unknown**

What's interesting is that because there are no people in Listfield's paintings, we assume the perspective of the astronaut, of the visitor. As we move through each painting, observing something we've seen before, we're also seeing it without our filter, through the eyes of a visitor. We see it without any narrative context. And it forces us to ask some new and different questions.

---

1. Check out his work at www.astronautdinosaur.com.

Who built this? And why did they build it this way?
What is this for? Was it helpful?
Who gathered here and what did they believe?

And so on and so forth. If I were to give an art school breakdown of these paintings, this is how I would frame what's happening: when we juxtapose a visitor, something out of context, into a familiar setting, it makes the narrative of the setting unknown. And it is in the *unknowing* of the narrative that wonder begins to appear.

Unknowing Is the Doorway to Wonder

Unknowing, or confronting the narrative, is the process of defamiliarizing yourself with something, allowing it to become new again. Unknowing takes what you already know and gives it a depth you never considered before.

This can happen when you watch a movie again, knowing now what the big twist at the end reveals—that the main character was dead, blind, or just a figment of someone's subconscious— and you see the movie in a whole new way. Or when you learn the backstory to a modern art piece, and it ceases to be just a bunch of circles and shapes but an artifact of a creative person's conversation with the entire history of art. Or when you decide to move from briefs to boxers, and khakis are no longer a casual, comfortable pant choice but an anxiety-ridden vestment of potential public embarrassment.

One of my favorite words that relates to this experience of unknowing is *ostranenie*. It means to defamiliarize from know-

ing something. According to Russian formalists who coined the term in the early 1900s, it is the central concept for any creative work. It is an artistic technique of presenting an audience with common things in an unfamiliar or bizarre way so they can gain a new perspective and see the world differently.

This is why poetry is so effective in illuminating ordinary life as a fantastic gift to experience. Mary Oliver's poem "The Summer Day" does just this. She describes ordinary activities like watching a grasshopper and lying in the grass as the key to bearing witness to the miracle of existence, and she asks us what we plan to do with our "one wild and precious life."[2] Through her simple yet calculated language, she is helping us see our ordinary lives as extraordinary. This is why art is so helpful. This is what is happening with the Scott Listfield paintings.

Wonder Hack

When we confront our assumptions, our preconceived narratives about whatever is before us—art, people, outcomes, and possibilities—we can begin to see our lives in a whole new way.

So here's the daily hack to get in touch with the filter of wonder:

Try to become a visitor to your own life every day.

Become an astronaut of wonder to your own existence. Imagine being the space explorer in the Scott Listfield paintings, walking around the artifacts of your life with no backstory to what any of them are. To help you with this imaginative exercise, you have a tool that can help you see with the eyes of a visitor. This tool is a question.

What don't I know?

---

2. Mary Oliver, *New and Selected Poems*, vol. 1 (Boston: Beacon, 1992), 94.

Whenever you find yourself bored with your life or depressed with the seemingly unchanging possibilities of it, stop and ask, *Well, what don't I know about this situation?* Look at your life from a visitor's point of view.

Wherever you find yourself right now, look up and imagine seeing everything for the first time.

What don't you know about the building you're in? Who designed it? Did they like or love the design? Who built it? How long did it take? Are there secrets in these walls? Did a broken-hearted construction worker write a bleeding-heart poem on the interior of these walls to the girl who just dumped him, only to cover it up with drywall and paint? Most likely not, but you don't know for sure.

Or what about the people all around you? What are the interior thoughts of each of them right now? What kinds of stories are here? How many people here have run a marathon? Who here has swum with dolphins?

Who here is contemplating shoplifting or quitting their job? Has anyone here seen a UFO? Or a ghost? What kinds of secrets are held by the people around you? I bet if you could see some of the secrets people hold, you'd be surprised how much spicier this room would be than you expected it to be.

"What don't I know?" is the key to unlock wonders around you. It causes you to look deeper into what you assume you know and find infinitely more happening than you could ever hope to understand or imagine. Especially about yourself.

What don't you know about you?

I'm on My Way

At the advice of my therapist, I started to pay attention to what I say to myself. My inner talk. My self-dialogue. She asked me to write it in a journal so I could see the ways I was placing myself in a certain kind of narrative.

At the time, I was working on a creative project and had come to a spot in the project I couldn't solve. I was in my studio at my sketch table, and I kept running through sketch after sketch after sketch with no resolution. With dozens of crumpled-up sketch-paper balls at my feet, I heard myself whisper in frustration, "I'm never going to be a great artist."

The words stopped me. I caught myself. What did I just say? "I'm never going to be a great artist." I just spoke a narrative about my life. Where did that conclusion come from?

So I began to unpack all the pieces of that statement. It wasn't hard to see where this argument came from. I don't have any formal art training. I'm mostly self-taught. I've never won any awards for art making. I've never sold a piece for oodles of money. Degrees, awards, and riches are all identifiers of success, and I had made these identifiers the marks of a successful artist. And according to my own invented rubric, I was not measuring up.

Our most limiting conclusions are always going to come to us in a sentence form where the subject "I" is followed by a negative qualifier: am *not*, am *never*, can*not*, do *not* . . .

Now that I had identified this narrative, I knew I needed to change it. I needed to find an alternative to the trajectory I assumed I was headed toward. I didn't need to overcompensate by bloating my ego and shouting, "I'm going to be the greatest artist ever!" We have Kanye West for that. I just needed to tweak the statement to give me room for growth and potential. I replaced "I'll never be a great artist" with "*I'm on my way* to becoming a great artist."

I'm on my way means that failing at something doesn't support the argument that I'm a failure. It just means I'm learning as I go. This isn't the end. *I'm on my way.* I'm getting better, and I can apply what I've learned in my next endeavor.

As an artist, I knew I needed something to help me remember. And because I like to make jokes, I made a coffee mug that reads "Future Famous Dead Artist."

I *am* on my way to becoming a great artist, but admittedly I'm part of a tradition in which success is typically accomplished after the artist dies. Patrons tend to buy our work after we've kicked the bucket.

It's a joke, yes, but it also helps me see my journey in the context of a larger community of artisans who have gone before me. I use this mug to hold my coffee in the morning. When I wake up in the morning, I make some delicious pour-over coffee, take a sip, look at my mug, and remember, "I'm on my way." It makes me giggle. But when I say, "I'm on my way," rather than "I'm never going to be," the trajectory of where I think I'm going is changed.

Our narrative, whatever it may be, is an argument built by assumptions. Assumptions are simply limited conclusions. Our narrative-making minds are putting together stories based on the limited information they have, and they are creating primitive conclusions that are keeping us safe, yes, but also preventing us from having a more expansive perspective. As we slowly begin to question each assumption and pull it apart, we can ask, "Where did I acquire this assumption? Whose voice is this? Is it mine or someone else's? Is this assumption a fact or just an opinion?" When we dismantle the argument by pulling apart all the assumptions, all of a sudden we open ourselves up to a universe of possibilities.

Tired of the Old Narrative

Admittedly, the content of this book was influenced by middle age. When I found myself crying on my toilet, I was approaching my fortieth birthday, and the age narratives were running wild. I know age is a number invented by our planetary orbit, but turning forty really does feel like approaching some kind of threshold. Like a crossing from one half to another. Like reaching the top of a hill and looking down at what's on the other side, only to find out it's your eventual death!

I know forty isn't old. But I feel like the dominant narrative in our culture is if we haven't figured out our lives when we're young, we're too late. If we aren't Taylor Swift and didn't figure out who we wanted to be at the age of fifteen, we'll never make anything great later on in our years on earth. This is a limited argument, but it might be true for music. Usually, bands or musicians hit it big when they're younger, and then in their twilight years they kind of fade from cultural relevance. A few stay relevant over their careers, but do we really like their latest work? We don't really want new music from the Backstreet Boys. "I Want It That Way" is just the right amount of late-nineties nostalgia.

I found myself close to forty and wondered, *Is there any more for me? Can I still accomplish and participate in works, rhythms, and endeavors that bring me to life? Can I start something new at this age and become really good at it?* Don't we all have a sneaking suspicion that as we get older, it's too late for us?

I started looking around for other people who were confronted with middle age, and I discovered that many, many people have encountered the same narratives. What they found was that there was much more to grow into! But they had to undo their narratives to enter a new and previously unimaginable possibility.

Paulo Coehlo didn't publish his first book, *The Pilgrimage*, until he was forty. He wrote *The Alchemist*, which is a great book, when he was forty-one. Published initially by a small Brazilian publishing house, *The Alchemist* was picked up by a major publisher several years later. It took about fifteen years after that to reach the *New York Times* bestseller list. Coehlo was sixty when this book finally became a *New York Times* bestseller!

Vera Wang didn't begin her designing career until the age of forty. Julia Child didn't write her first cookbook until she was forty-nine. Stan Lee didn't have his first comic book hit, *Fantastic Four*, until he was just shy of his thirty-ninth birthday. Henry Ford introduced the Model T to the world when he was forty-five.

Samuel Jackson has been a Hollywood staple for years now, but he'd had only bit parts before landing an award-winning role at age forty-three in Spike Lee's film *Jungle Fever* in 1991. If he would've given up on acting while he was in his thirties, we would live in a universe without *Snakes on a Plane*! And I can't imagine what a sad universe that would be.

Anna Mary Robertson Moses, better known as Grandma Moses, began her prolific painting career at seventy-eight. In 2006, one of her paintings sold for $1.2 million. Rodney Dangerfield didn't start doing regular comedy acts until he was in his forties, and then he finally made it on *The Ed Sullivan Show* at forty-six. Leslie Jones didn't make it on *Saturday Night Live* until she was forty-seven, and she was one of the best cast members ever! Jack Weil was forty-five when he founded what became the most popular Western wear brand, Rockmount Ranch Wear. He remained its CEO until he died at the ripe old age of 107 in 2008.

All of these people had to address their narratives about themselves as they were getting older and say, "I'm not done. It's not too late for me. There's something more for me."

In other words, all these people looked the T-Rex of Giving Up straight in the eye and boldly declared, "You're wrong. Change is possible. I'm on my way!"

The truth is that "nothing's gonna change" until we're willing to confront the narratives that keep us from changing. This is an incredibly hard commitment to make because these narratives are there to keep us "safe," or at least to make us believe we are. My hope is that you're reading this book because you're tired of these narratives, which is a good thing. You need to get tired of them—so tired of them that you'll do anything to bust out of these limited conclusions.

So unknow your narrative. Begin to pull apart the assumptions that are building that narrative. When you do, you may be surprised at how you see your life. You may start to see that what seemed to be your biggest vulnerability is the way you can now access a universe of unforeseen possibilities.

Chapter 7

The Light of Failure

Once upon a time a great ship was built. It was strong, mighty, and something to behold. It was given a great purpose: to deliver important seeds to the far side of the ocean. The ship cele-

brated its great purpose. It thought, *How great a task I have! I must be valuable. This is what I was meant to do.*

So it set sail on the great sea.

On its journey an unforeseen storm came upon it. It thought

it could handle it. It was sure it could handle it. But the storm was much bigger than it had anticipated or planned for. It couldn't control the situation. The ship was wiped out by the storm.

It found itself wrecked on some rocks. It couldn't move. It couldn't go anywhere. The great ship was lost in the ocean, and it sat there for a long time with its failure—its failure to fulfill its purpose.

But something unexpected happened. Slowly the water seeped into the seeds, and they began to germinate and grow. They grew and grew, and over time a large forest emerged.

One day, another ship came passing by, also broken and floundering

ing because of an unforeseen storm. It came to the broken ship's island and asked, "May I rest here awhile? I'm so tired from my journey."

The great ship replied, "Sure. By all means."

As the newly arrived ship rested, the great ship gave some of its wood to build a shelter for its crew. They stayed awhile, and after they had rested up and the ship was restored, the visiting ship left, renewed for its journey.

"Thank you for your hospitality! You really helped me," said the restored ship to the great ship.

After a while another ship passed by. That ship also asked

if it could rest for a time. It too had been bruised and battered by an unforeseen storm. It needed a place to recover. The great ship took more of its wood and built a shelter for the much larger crew. When that ship was healed, it also went on its way.

This cycle kept happening. New ship after new ship kept coming, all of them injured because of an unexpected storm and needing a place to recover. The great ship realized it had something to give—a place for rest and a sense of solidarity with ships that had been wrecked because of unforeseen storms on the great sea.

Eventually, the great ship decided to build a lighthouse so that all ships passing by that way could be cared for, find rest, and then continue on their journey.

Throughout the years, the great ship cared for many, many bruised and broken ships. Over time, the ship came to recognize a puzzling mystery: *out of its own wreckage and failure, it became a gift to others.*

It always wondered if this was its purpose all along.

Chapter 8

Bliss
Is a
Process

The death of a dream is like the shipwreck. The vulnerability found in the shipwreck is the failure to accomplish what we thought we were supposed to do, supposed to achieve, supposed to be. The wreck is where the narratives stopped working for us and left us painfully vulnerable on the great sea.

Yet the unforeseen gift of this new vulnerability is that it has placed us in a position where we are open for a change. A change of perspective. A change of identity. A change of possibility. This moment, this shipwreck, is just one part of our story. It's not the end of our story, but the surprising opening to something unforeseen. And we must go deep down into the hidden seeds of desire in us to find what wants to come forth now that the dream has died.

I'm on my way is a powerful mental health and spiritual practice in combating the narrative that nothing can change. The power comes from its ability to offer us grace in *this* moment of our lives. The grace of perspective that we're still in process. The grace that our story isn't over and we're not done yet. The grace that there are unforeseen possibilities just ahead of us. The grace that it's not all up to us.

Also, *I'm on my way* is a powerful practice because it puts us in a relational context with our deepest desire. I'm on my way . . . to what? To where? To whom? *What is it that I want to be on my way toward?* Developing a certain skill or craft? Starting a dream business? Repairing broken relationships? Deepening a faith? Healing trauma? Changing vocations?

You can be on your way today. In fact, you are on your way right now.

Pursuing Your Bliss

So let me ask you this: *What do you want to do?*

For many, specifically in the context of work, this question is frustratingly paralyzing. At a certain time in history, people had very limited options in choosing a vocation, so this choice was already made for them. If your dad was a stone mason, you'd probably be one too. If you were born into the priesthood, you were most likely going into the priesthood. If you were born with extra fingers and toes, you were most likely joining an ancient version of the Barnum & Bailey Circus.

But for us in modern times, the vocational possibilities are endless, and we are paralyzed by all the choices. We've heard the stories of wealthy Wall Street traders leaving their exhausting New York City jobs to start a more peaceful and satisfying life as a canoeing tour guide along the Colorado River, but we are left wondering if we should start by making a lot of money in a soul-sucking job and then eventually quit to do what we really want to do, or just get to what we hope to do now. Or we see these cool kids on Instagram taking pictures of themselves on abandoned wooden bridges in slobby chic outfits and find out that they make six-figure salaries and we think, *Should I buy more sweatpants and find more abandoned bridges so I can become an influencer?*

We are paralyzed by choice, yes, but we're also deeply afraid of choosing the wrong career and regretting it later. We'll get to regret later in the book, but let me point to a good starting place to know what you want to do: *you're going to have to trust your heart.*

You're going to have to pay attention to the desire that is already in you. You're going to need to believe the truth that this desire is there for a reason. That your desire points to a divine path placed within you for you to walk.

How do you begin to clue in on what your deepest desire is? Start by answering these few questions:

1. When was the last time I felt really alive?
2. When was the last time I did something so invigorating that hours seemed like minutes?
3. What was the last experience that made me think, *Could I do this as a job?*
4. What were the particulars that made me feel this way?

The answer to these questions will point to your bliss. *Your bliss is the feeling of being most alive.* Feeling the most like you— the truest you. The rapturous experience of being alive. This is the signpost for what you need to be pursuing.

Wanting Something from Life

I didn't stop being an artist after my "crying on the toilet" revelation. The narrative of what kind of artist I had hoped to be was failing, but I knew I still wanted to do creative work. I just wanted to do a different version of what I was doing. So I looked back at all I had done in my career and asked myself, *What projects have given me the most life? What experiences have given me the most bliss?* When I brought those key questions to all my work, a thread emerged—that it all involved performance in front of a live audience. And right when I zeroed in on that, the T-Rex of Giving Up showed up. The T-Rex always shows up to stand in the way of what makes a person come alive the most. But now that I could see my bliss, I knew I needed to face the monster that was standing in the way of it.

I'm on my way to becoming that kind of artist. I simply needed to start walking the path. I needed to start *wanting* something from my life.

You need to start wanting something from your life again.

This may sound like a recipe for repeating pain. You may feel you've already done this and it didn't work out; hence, the death of a dream. Beloved, you must pick up your dreams again, but this time leave out your preconceived notion of what it's supposed to look like. Get in touch with that deep desire inside you. You need to be *on your way* to something again.

From the beginning of our marriage, my wife has posed these questions periodically:

If I win the lottery tomorrow and never have to worry about money again, what would I do with my time?

What kind of job would I want?

Where would I live?

What would my friends be like?

Who would I hang out with?

What would I want to learn?

What would I do with my time?

How would I feel during the day?

Seriously, grab a piece of paper and answer these questions. Or just jot down your answers in the margins. Get really specific with your answers and use concrete examples.

Done? Good.

Now here's the twist on starting to dream again. I want you to take that list and ignore the outcomes of what you listed (money, fame, big house, and so on). I know, I sound crazy at this moment. I just told you to list concrete examples. What a tease I am! I want you to focus less on the outcomes and final destinations, and I want you to list the qualities of the kind of person who exists in these outcomes.

I'll give you an example. Let's say you wrote down, "I want to live in a house by the beach"—which is what I would write down because that's where I hope to be one day. What are the qualities of the kind of person who lives in a house by the beach? If I'm being honest, my first thought was, *Living by the beach is expensive, so I'd have to be the kind of person who makes a good amount of money.* Maybe you had that thought too, but that's not a quality; that's an outcome. You really don't know how much money you'll make in the future, so let's sidestep that narrative. *Who would you be if you lived in a house by the beach?*

For me, I love surfing. It brings me alive and restores and heals my soul on the worst days. So I'd like to make time for that kind of practice in my life. I grew up around the ocean, and the smells and sounds give me a deep sense of belonging. I'd like to be the kind of person who rests in their belonging. I'd like to have a good work-life habit. I'd like to be the kind of person who works hard, yes, but who also makes time to enjoy living. And so on and so forth.

Recap: I'd like to be the kind of person . . .

who makes time for restorative practices,
who rests in their belonging,
who has a work-life habit.

Question: Do I have to wait to be this kind of person until I get a house by the beach? Or can I start being that kind of person now? Must I rely on the purchase of a particular house to be the kind of person I'd like to be, or can I start practicing those qualities right where I'm at? Let's take it a step further. Is it the house by the beach that makes me who I am, or is it who I already am that makes the house by the beach my dream scenario?

Let's take it to a vocational scenario. Say someone wants to be a public speaker. They want to speak to large crowds about things they care about. They imagine how cool it would be to be a motivational speaker. Okay, great! Let's leave the outcomes aside for a second and ask what the qualities of a public speaker are. *Someone who has something to say. Someone who has developed their own unique and personal way of communicating. Someone who is participating in life and translating their wisdom gained through experience by means of an auditory medium.* Do you need a large audience to begin that work? Or can you start participating in these qualities now? You can start paying attention to the particulars of life and seek to find the corporate wisdom today. You don't need a large crowd to begin being that type of person, but you must be *that type of person* for a large crowd to be interested in listening to you.

Not Feeling Different

The purpose of this exercise is to expose the myth that the *outcome* will satisfy your deepest desire. We may think that once we reach our concrete outcomes, we will feel different, which is what we really want in our present situation. To feel different than I do now (cozy feeling suit). To feel like I'm not stuck here (vehicle of destiny). To feel like I can be the kind of person I hoped to be (tuning fork).

But I'm here to tell you that concrete outcomes won't give you those results. The truth is that none of us know the exact shape our lives will take in the future. Our lives have many unforeseen surprises in store for us. Some joyful. Some tragic. What tripped us up in the death of our dream were the invented specifics we found ourselves not accomplishing. We must dream again to push past the T-Rex of Giving Up, but this time we must hold the concrete outcomes loosely. Specific outcomes can be important because they give us a direction to walk. But becoming the kind of person we hope to be is in the journey of walking again.

In 2016, a few months after the December 2015 release of the much-anticipated *Star Wars: The Force Awakens*, director J. J. Abrams and fellow director Dan Trachtenberg sat down with *The Nerdist Podcast* host Chris Hardwick for a discussion of numerous topics, including Dan's latest film *10 Cloverfield Lane*, for which J. J. had been the producer. Since J. J. had just come off the success of a well-received Star Wars film, Chris asked him what it had been like to direct a Star Wars film.

> **Chris Hardwick:** Is there any kind of weird postpartum after doing something of that scale, where you, probably your whole life, you go, "Wow, that would be the ultimate," and then you do it and it goes well, so what do you feel afterward?
>
> **J. J. Abrams:** Well, I'll tell you what it is. It's a funny thing, and you just brought up *Taking Care of Business*. I remember my whole life, since I was eight or nine, wanting to be a filmmaker, and it was just this thing that I just knew, if I was lucky enough to get the shot, would be how I'd want to live my life. Whether I could or not, you know, I didn't know. But it was the thing I wanted forever.

And there's that thing that happened for me, and I'm sure we all have our versions of this, that you kinda think, *Okay, that's somehow the finish line, that's the place you want to get to*, and when you get there, you will have become that person, that thing. You will have reached a certain level of insight or evolution or whatever, that you will feel like, *I have become that person*.

And I remember when I was in my last year of college and I ran into a friend, Jill Mazursky, and we came up with an idea, and we ended up writing it and then selling this pitch to Disney, and it was *Taking Care of Business*. And I remember signing these documents and getting paid, and I was suddenly a professional screenwriter. And I remember the feeling of not feeling different, and how weird that was.

And then I remember when the movie actually got made, I thought, *Okay, I'll see my name on the screen*, and I remember feeling no different and thinking that's weird . . .

It's interesting that you bring this up because I feel like I have now gone through this kind of gauntlet, and I was lucky enough to get the opportunity. I was lucky enough to be part of that movie and work with all those people, and we were all lucky enough to have it go as well as it did. I sit here the way I would have sat here, you know, ten years ago, the way I will probably sit here ten years from now. It's like, there is not that moment where you go, *Oh, it feels different*.

I don't know about you, but whether it's a thing I've written or a thing that I have directed, or whatever it is, I know I've done it, and I can talk about the process, but it's somehow impossible that it's happened because when you get to the other side of it, you're the same exact person, you know. Our experiences shape us a little bit, of course, but I just, honestly, I feel gratitude that I'm sitting here at all, and that I got to be part of something that was as much fun as *The Force Awakens*.[1]

It blows my mind that J. J. Abrams has never felt different after any one of his accomplishments. But he's felt immense gratitude having gone through the process.

What process would you want to be grateful for having gone through?

Accomplishment often doesn't deliver the feeling of success you want it to bring. I remember having a mixture of emotions on the release day of my first solo book, *Honest Advent*. I was relieved, excited, nervous, and, lastly, disappointed. I was disappointed on the day my book was available in bookstores everywhere! Why? Because it didn't fill me in the way I thought it might. But to echo what J. J. Abrams said, I found myself immensely grateful for having been able to go through the whole process. It was the process of doing that made me the kind of person I always wanted to be—a published author.

The Road Trip Process

One of the narratives we need to unknow in not giving up on ourselves is the destination is the goal. It's not. It's partaking in the

---

1. "J. J. Abrams and Dan Trachtenberg," *Nerdist Podcast*, March 11, 2016, http://nerdist.nerdistind.libsynpro.com/jj-abrams-and-dan-trachtenberg.

bliss that's pointing us in that direction, and the transformation of self that happens when we practice our bliss.

Think about it this way: let's say you were going on a road trip, and you weren't sure you were going to make it to the destination. How would that change the route you'd take? You'd probably choose a route that was likely as enjoyable as the destination. That you'd realize it wasn't all about getting somewhere, but more about what happens to you in the process of getting somewhere.

If you didn't know how it was all going to turn out or even if you'd reach that destination, *what trip would you like to go on in your life?* What process would you like to participate in? What journey would be blissful, no matter whether or not it led to any kind of accomplishment?

"I'm on my way." What is the *way* you want to be on?

This consideration is helpful when we begin to lay out our future goals because the look and shape of the actual destination may not be anything we can predict. Sometimes it can be helpful not to be too specific in describing our outcomes because the process of following our bliss may lead us to an unexpected outcome. Naming concrete outcomes could actually diminish the potential of what we are becoming.

I'm on my way . . . to . . .

I'm adamant about this because the question we often get asked—"Where do you want to be in five years?"—really freaks me out. My response is always, "You mean if aliens don't show up and change everything?" Because if they do and they're looking for interstellar recruits to explore the galaxy, I'm leaving this performance artist career and heading for the stars!

I joke, but it's my way of keeping an open hand on what can happen in my life that might change everything in my life.

My friend Katherine Wolf was a budding actor and model at the age of twenty-six. She and her husband, Jay, and their six-month-old baby were living in a house in Malibu, California, when she suffered an arteriovenous malformation rupture that caused a brain stroke, leading to a loss of fine motor coordination, double vision, deafness, and facial paralysis. This changed Katherine's and Jay's lives radically in ways they never could have imagined. But it has also led them into a work they never would have imagined. Many years after her stroke, Katherine and Jay now lead two sessions of Hope Heals camp each summer for families affected by disabilities. They travel all over and speak to thousands of people, inviting them into the hope found in redefining what it means to live a rich life. They have published two amazing books about hope and suffering[2] and are some of the greatest people I've ever encountered. But where they ended up in life was unexpected.

Where we'll end up in five years will be unexpected. But here's what I know about where I'd like to be in five years: I hope in five years to be still pursuing my bliss, which is creative expression. I'm unclear about where all of this is going and what it all will look like, but I'm very clear on being the kind of person who is committed to a blissful rhythm five, ten, twenty years from now. This commitment is important because throughout my life, I've had various occupations. I've worked in the food service industry.

---

2. Katherine and Jay Wolf, *Hope Heals: A True Story of Overwhelming Loss and an Overcoming Love* (Grand Rapids: Zondervan, 2016); Katherine and Jay Wolf, *Suffer Strong: How to Survive Anything by Redefining Everything* (Grand Rapids: Zondervan, 2020).

I've worked in the nonprofit sector. I've been a vocational minister. I've worked at a design and branding company. In all of those occupations, though, I was still committed to following my bliss. We can maintain our commitment to our bliss wherever we find ourselves.

"I'm on my way."

To what, to where, to whom do you want to be on your way to?

Because the vulnerable you right now is part of that journey. You're not done yet. Nor are you alone in your process. Those broken ships in the shipwreck lighthouse story helped the shipwrecked ship find its true calling. It's not all up to you to figure out. Do you believe that? Or do you think you're all on your own? Because if you think it's all up to you, then this is the perfect place to have a DTR[3] with the Divine.

---

3. "Define the relationship."

Chapter 9

DTR with the Divine

Two stories.

The first is a familiar story that has found its way into songs, musicals, and even major motion pictures. It's the story of Joseph, his brothers, and his technicolor dreamcoat from the Hebrew book of Genesis. It's a very long story, so I'll just touch on the highlights.

Joseph's jealous brothers fake his death and sell him into slavery. He winds up in Egypt working for a guy named Potiphar. Joseph is so good at his job that he wins Potiphar's trust. But Mrs. Potiphar has the sexy eyes for Joe and makes a move, only to see Joe run away, leaving his coat behind. Peeved at being denied, Mrs. P. tells Mr. P. that Joe made a move on her. She shows him the coat, and Mr. P. throws Joe into jail. He's there for three years. He's so good at being in jail that he wins the guards' trust. He gives some prophecies to some cellmates, which later becomes fortuitous for him because one of his cellmates gets his old job back in Pharaoh's court. Pharaoh is having some disturbing dreams and needs someone to translate them for him. The former cellmate remembers Joe and tells Pharaoh about him. Joe gets called up and nails his interview with the correct dream analysis. He knocks it out of the park so much that Pharaoh makes him his VP over the whole land and puts him in charge of preparing the country for an impending famine.

Next scene. The famine is upon everyone. Joseph's brothers go to Egypt to find food, and they get an audience with Joseph. They don't recognize him, but he recognizes them. Except there is one new member to the group—his younger brother Benjamin, born of the same mom. (His other brothers were from other mothers. Good ol' biblical polygamy!) And then it's written:

> And as he raised his eyes and saw his brother Benjamin, his mother's son, he said, "Is this your youngest brother, of whom you spoke to me?" Then he said, "May God be gracious to you, my son." Joseph then hurried out, for he was deeply stirred over his brother, and he looked for a place to weep; so he entered his chamber and wept there. (Genesis 43:29–30 NASB)

He looks for a place to cry. Like a bedroom. A coat closet. Even a bathroom (wink). Someplace where he could be alone to try to manage how he feels about things not turning out the way he expected. Sounds familiar.

Joseph sends the brothers on their way back home but has secretly placed a valuable chalice in one of their grain sacks. The Egyptian cops search the bags, find the stolen chalice, and bring back the brothers. There's a whole "he said, she said" scenario that's interesting but not essential to this chapter, because it all leads to this moment:

> Then Joseph could no longer control himself before all his attendants, and he cried out, "Have everyone leave my presence!" So there was no one with Joseph when he made himself

known to his brothers. And *he wept so loudly that the Egyptians heard him*, and Pharaoh's household heard about it.

Joseph said to his brothers, "I am Joseph! Is my father still living?" But his brothers were not able to answer him, because they were terrified at his presence.

Then Joseph said to his brothers, "Come close to me." When they had done so, he said, "I am your brother Joseph, the one you sold into Egypt! And now, do not be distressed and do not be angry with yourselves for selling me here, because it was to save lives that God sent me ahead of you. For two years now there has been famine in the land, and for the next five years there will be no plowing and reaping. But God sent me ahead of you to preserve for you a remnant on earth and to save your lives by a great deliverance." (Genesis 45:1–7, emphasis added)

Again with the crying. I like the crying parts of the Bible. There aren't too many of them, but they're all my favorites.

In this story we have two big crying moments. One in a moment of grief—the loss of the way Joseph hoped his life would go. Another in a moment of seeing what was happening behind the scenes. Seeing an unforeseen story line unfold in the midst of a seemingly random series of disappointing and amazing events. Realizing a divine participation was at work through the whole thing.

Story two.

When I was in my mid-twenties, I crossed the Atlantic Ocean and lived in Europe for ten months. For three of those months, I backpacked all over Europe with various friends in magical places. For seven months, I attended two Torchbearers Bible schools—one in England for the winter semester, and one in Austria for the spring semester.

The Bible school in England is called Capernwray. It's in northern England in the Lake District, a fairly rural part of England, consisting of quaint little towns and a lot of sheep. Around 250 students from more than thirty countries go to school in a large castle-like structure. It's technically referred to as a chateau, but to us Yanks it looked like a straight-up castle from a Jane Austen novel. Like a mini Hogwarts but without any magical talking paintings.

Most of the student body are between eighteen and twenty-two years old. I was on the older side at twenty-four, but a smattering of students were in their thirties and forties, even a few in their fifties and sixties. One of these sexagenarians was a woman named Rita. She was like one of the castle grandmothers. Kind and sweet, with a joyous presence and a nonstop smile. At first, you'd think she was just a nice woman from a small Texas town. But after I got to know her, I found her story was much more complicated than that.

Rita had recently become a widow. Her husband had died earlier in the year from a long-drawn-out battle with cancer. Even though Rita was surrounded by her adult children and her lovely grandbabies, she said that everywhere in her small town reminded her of her husband, and it was driving her crazy. She needed to get outta Dodge for a while, so she signed up to go to a Bible school as far away as she could without needing to know another language. Thus rural England, a substantial distance from Dodge.

In the main entrance of the castle, underneath the grand staircase, was a little sitting nook where Rita would often sit. You could find her reading or journaling there, but she was always open to an interruption. One morning I found her journaling, and I asked if I could join her for a bit. We chatted about the latest castle happenings and school projects we were working on, and then I asked what she was writing about. She said she was just thinking about all of us young people and the unexpected roads lying before us. She said she was writing a prayer for all of us. Instantly curious, I asked if she could share with me what she had written, and here it is:

Don't mess with Jesus

I pray for all these beautiful young people and tremble at
the world they face—

> *tremble for the joy, the sorrow, the glory, and the pain.*
> *But what a blessing their lives could be if only they knew*
how safe they are in God's hands.
> *They could live with passion and abandon to Him,*
> *not being bound up with success, money, fear of the*
future, fear of relationships, fear of failure. They could live
freely, and in such joy, if they only knew the truth about
living:
> *Give it to Jesus, and then give it everything you've got!*
> *It will be glorious and painful;*
> *you will get wounded in the Fight,*
> *but you'll come back stronger than ever;*
> *and someday*
> *you'll look back and say,*
"I'd do it all over again, Lord! It was awesome!"

Rita said she would do it all over again. The twists and the
turns. The marriage and the eventual death. The getting wounded
in the fight. Why?

Awakening to the Already

I don't know what you think about God. I don't know if you believe
or don't believe or kind of, sort of, sometimes believe. Where we
grew up in the world, what kind of community we grew up in,
and what our parents are like all affect how we think about God.
Sometimes it feels like talking about God is just discussing our

own thoughts about the mystery of how life works. As comedian Pete Holmes says, "A great quote that I love is, 'God is the name of the blanket we put over the mystery to give it shape' . . . We're trying to talk about something undiscussable."[1]

This book does not try to convince you of what God is like. There are endless writings from sages, mystics, gurus, and theologians that can scratch that itch for you. But I want to invite you to what I have found to be true: that a spiritual life is not about getting God's attention; *a spiritual life is about awakening to the voice and the work of God that are already in your life.*

When we experience the death of a dream, one of the narratives that can easily trip us up is that God has left us to do this on our own. Or that the Almighty had a plan for us, but we messed it up. Or that the Giver of our existence just stopped being involved in our existence. That we're really just on our own. But what I can attest to in my life, in Rita's life, in technicolor Joe's life, is that there are divine behind-the-scenes workings that you have no idea about, and when they reveal themselves in an unforeseen future, it'll bring you to tears.

To not give up on ourselves in the moment when our dreams are dying, we must hold on to the reality that we are not done. That the end of the dream is not the finale but just a chapter in a long book that's still being written. And besides you, the other coauthor of this book is the Giver of you.

"I'm on my way" . . . but not alone.

Transformation is a twofold process. For parts of it, you are

---

1. Quoted in Alexa Edwards, "Going Holmes," *Relevant*, October 12, 2017, www.relevantmagazine.com/culture/going-holmes.

in charge, and for other parts, you are not. You can read more, volunteer at a local food bank, and decline seconds on hot fudge sundaes if you want to transform your mind, soul, and body. You have agency to change. But for other aspects of becoming the kind of person you'd like to be, you aren't in charge. You will find yourself in situations that you would never choose for yourself but that will leave you irrevocably transformed. Yes, like car accidents, strokes, and job losses, but also situations that can only be healed through the awakening of love, hope, and forgiveness within you. These transform us too, and the Divine is in the business of transformation.

Two Graces

I wish I could, but I really can't convince you that God is already involved in your life. You must examine this for yourself. I could tell you story after story, but until it's *your* story, it just seems like I'm telling you a fairy tale. But I can offer you a couple of practices to help you start tapping into this Divine participation. One has to do with your soul, and the other has to do with your body.

Again, the comedian Pete Holmes (I'm a fan—what can I say?) has a great bit in which he tries to get the audience to tap into the mystery of having a soul and a body. I was at one of his live standup shows where he asked the audience to take a moment to check if we had to pee or not. He paused. We all checked. And then he shouted in his goofy, inquisitive voice, "What is that?" So funny. We take it for granted, but we can do that!

In the same vein of checking if you have to pee or not, I would like you to say something to God. A prayer. A whazzup. A request. A thank-you. Whatever you want. But I don't want you to say something with audible words that come out of your mouth; I want you to communicate with your very being. Think it. Feel it. Emote it.

Take a moment to do it now.

(Come back when you're ready.)

What did you just do? What is that? Somehow, inside our very being is a kind of portal that allows us to talk directly to God. A door that can open and close. I like to use the metaphor of a telephone. We have a soul telephone connected to the Giver of our soul.

Where did you get that telephone? Did someone come along and place that telephone inside you? Did you go to a store, a shrine, or a sanctuary and pick one out? Did you have to beg, yell, or plead to get it? Or has it always been inside you? The answer is it's always been there. From the very beginning of your existence, you've had a telephone. It's a gift that has always been there. The word we have for getting something we didn't have to request, earn, or purchase is *grace*. We have a grace inside us in the form of a telephone.

Sidenote. You have a telephone. I have a telephone. Everyone has a telephone. It's interesting to see this metaphor because in the history of religion people have believed that they needed to walk around and put telephones in others, which is silly. It's already there! You can't put in what's already in. Humans can definitely ignore their telephone, and, in fact, a good definition of spiritual formation is "paying attention to your telephone." What if we were to lay down any feeling that it's on us to pass out telephones, and instead get curious with everyone we meet about what kind of phone calls they're having? What do they talk about? That sounds so much more interesting.

You also have another grace inside you. You have a grace for your soul and a grace for your body.

I want you to find your heartbeat. Put your hand on your chest and find the beat that is happening right underneath your rib cage. Or if that's not possible, you can place your fingers on your neck or wrist, wherever the blood is pumping through an easy-to-access artery. Just find that beat. Sit with it for a time.

Take as long as you need.

Where did you get this heart? Did someone come along and place it inside you? Did you go to a store, a shrine, or a sanctuary and pick one out? Did you have to beg, yell, or plead to get it? Or has it always been inside you? I think you see where this is going.

It's always been there. It's part of your being. Your heart beats, pumping life-giving blood throughout your body without you even thinking about it. You're not in charge of it. You're alive right now by something you're not in charge of. Your life is sustained by grace. It's nothing you've ever had to ask for.

We can take it a step further and look at our breath. Yes, we can control our breath, but our breathing is mostly an involuntary activity. It too reflects a sustaining by grace.

We can take a big step out and look at our planet. Our planet is perfectly positioned around the sun in order for life to happen below its stratosphere. All life—my life, your life—is sustained by an orbit we are not in charge of. Again, another grace.

How many graces are there in your life? How many graces are you aware of? How many graces are you not aware of?

Technicolor Joe wept so loudly that the Egyptians heard him because he was awakened to the unforeseen grace that had been working in his life. He didn't see it when he was betrayed by his brothers. He didn't see it when he was thrown in jail for something he was wrongly accused of. He didn't even see it when he got the promotion of a lifetime. He saw it when he realized all of those experiences uniquely prepared him for the place where he found himself.

The prayer Rita wrote is about that too. It isn't filled with shallow pleasantries that life will be hard at times, but "Just keep being positive, kids!" It was written with the full awareness that life has joys and disappointments, loves and heartbreaks, risks and rewards, births and deaths. But on the other side of all that, her blessing to us "young'uns" was to show that what makes life worth living is befriending the grace that has been with us all along.

Find the heartbeat. Find the telephone.

Give yourself some grace by embracing the truth that it's not all up to you.

Give yourself some grace by embracing the truth that you're not done yet.

Give yourself some grace as you realize that you too, as your life unfolds, can be the kind of person who journals under a castle staircase, "I'd do it all over again, Lord! It was awesome!"

The Second Argument

Chapter 10

You Suck and Are Ugly

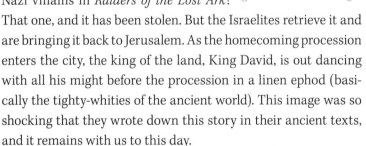

here's a weird story in the ancient Hebrew Scriptures that goes like this:

The ark of the covenant has been stolen . . . you know, the one that melted off all the faces of the Nazi villains in *Raiders of the Lost Ark*? That one, and it has been stolen. But the Israelites retrieve it and are bringing it back to Jerusalem. As the homecoming procession enters the city, the king of the land, King David, is out dancing with all his might before the procession in a linen ephod (basically the tighty-whities of the ancient world). This image was so shocking that they wrote down this story in their ancient texts, and it remains with us to this day.

Here is what the account says: "As the ark of the LORD was entering the City of David. Michal daughter of Saul [David's wife] watched from a window. And when she saw King David leaping and dancing before the LORD, she despised him in her heart" (2 Samuel 6:16).

Let's break this down.

The ark of the covenant. A physical representation of a covenant between the people of Israel and YHWH, the Creator of all. The Giver of existence. Existence itself. A symbol of Existence itself is coming into their midst, and someone is dancing with all their might in the presence of Existence, and somebody else is standing on the sidelines despising the person who is dancing.

How do you become somebody who knows how to dance in the presence of Existence, and then how do you become the person who stands on the sidelines and despises those who have figured out how to dance?

Why We Make Superheroes

I think we should start by talking about superheroes. Have you seen that latest superhero film? Do you notice I don't even have to give a name to it? We're in a unique time in history when multiple superhero films come out every year—every month even! Hollywood has figured out how to make billions off comic books, so it's just one after the other, after the other, and I love it.

But I was reading a story to my son recently, and a centaur was in it. He asked, "What's a centaur?" I told him that a centaur is half human and half horse. It's a sort of ancient superhero. Back then, people didn't think about laser beams coming out of their eyes, or cutlery out of their hands. They just looked around the world and said, "What's big? Horses! Let's be half of that." That's how they made the centaur.

Then my son asked, "Do centaurs have outfits like superheroes do?" This is a tough question because I'm not exactly sure how centaurs would wear pants.

I think the complication comes with having two rib cages.

I'm bringing up superheroes and centaurs because from the very beginning of human existence, we have been making up superhero stories. When we look down the path of life and see what it's going to take to have success in our life, our immediate conclusion is:

We need to be more.

Wonder woman. *Super* man. *Bat* girl. A supplemental adjective is always tacked onto the subject because we're convinced that the subject on its own is not enough.

Path of Success

I believe each of us has a destination of success we would like to get to. "Success" can have a range of definitions, from how much money you make, to how large of an audience comes to see you, to how many vacations you have scheduled in your calendar year. Each of us has a personal definition of success that has sent us walking down a path toward our goal. But as we start to walk that path toward success, we are immediately confronted with the thought that we don't have what it takes to make it to that success.

The T-Rex of Giving Up whispers, "You suck and are ugly," meaning, you don't have what it takes to be successful, and there is something wrong with you out of your control that is always going to keep you from getting to that success.

I'm not smart enough.

I don't have the right education.

I don't have the right connections.

I don't have the right looks, voice, body, brains, money, resources to get to where I want to go.

I need to be more.

And we invent a caricature self, a superhero version of ourselves, and imagine if we were that version, we'd finally be able to get to the success we want. Obviously, these are made-up characters. Comic book illustrations brought to life by movie studios run by the grown-ups who used to read those comics. We're not comparing ourselves to real people. None of us would ever say we're literally trying to be a superhero. Except YouTuber Casey Neistat. I'm pretty sure he's a superhero.

What we actually have are idealistic versions of ourselves we think we need to be embedded in the real people we compare ourselves to. If you want to discover what your secret list of "not enough" consists of, just think about the people you compare yourself to. Usually the person you compare yourself with is someone on a path similar to the one you're on. You're walking down your path of success, and you glance over and see someone else who is leaps and bounds ahead of you. You think, *How did they get so far ahead in the direction I'm headed? What do they have that I don't have?* We try to step off our path and onto theirs, and thus we begin a comparative conversation.

Comparative Conversations

For years I've had a secret comparative conversation with a celebrity I've never told anyone about. At one time he was the bee's knees, but he's done some fairly ridiculous things of late, and I'd like to tell you I was freed of this comparison a few years ago. But for the longest time, my secret comparative conversation was with rapper and fashionista Kanye West.

The comparison started the only time I met Kanye, which was backstage at the Sasquatch! Music Festival in Washington State. He had just finished his *Graduation* set, which is a great album, and I had backstage passes and was hanging out in the beer garden. He came offstage and was walking to his trailer, while people were snapping selfies with him as he walked. I grabbed one with him—you can see in the photo that he was as happy as I was for the chance to get a photo together—and that was it! That's the only time we've ever met.

But a little while later, I found out Kanye and I are the same age. Our birthdays are only a few months apart. So because of something as simple as a number, anytime I found myself in a situation where my life wasn't going the way I hoped it would and I thought I was the problem, I would think, *I wonder what Kanye is up to. He's the same age as me. What should I be accomplishing?* And I would begin a comparative conversation with Mr. West.

I would see that he is very fashionable. He has his own shoe and clothing line. He exudes a casual sophistication and seems very confident in the clothes he wears. I'm a grown adult who is capable of buying any clothes I want, and even now I'm still not comfortable in the clothes I'm wearing.

He's a performer and sells out stadiums and arenas worldwide to adoring fans. Not too long ago I had six people show up to a performance I was doing in rural Minnesota. So basically the same kind of audience draw.

Kanye says things on TV that influence culture. I mean, we're talking about him right now! He's a celebrity, and he is in our lives because of television. I've been on TV once. The single greatest thing I may ever be known for is that I was on the game show *The Price Is Right*. With the original host, Bob Barker. Not only did I get called to Contestant's Row, but I also made it up onstage as a contestant. I bid on a prize, got to spin the wheel, won the wheel spin, made it to the Showcase Showdown, and was the grand prize winner of the show due to the overbidding of my adversary. I actually won *The Price Is Right*! I've lived all your game show fantasies. So maybe I beat Kanye in this instance.

We all have our secret comparisons. Who shows up in yours? Is it a celebrity? A mentor? A friend of a friend? Or just some stranger whose crazy-cool life you've seen on the internet?

The internet. Social media. We are in the age of social media, and this age has advanced a comparative narrative more than any other. Look, I'm not here to pooh-pooh social media. You're probably reading this book because of social media, and thank you for your support! There are definitely some positive aspects of social media, but other aspects are messing us up.

What's messing us up is *the curation of perfection that is very hard to recreate in real life.* You want to have a Pinterest-worthy wedding, but you're not in control of the humidity that day that makes all the bridesmaids' dresses cling to every crevice of the human body and adds a lot of pinching, pulling, and butt-cheek tugging as an unforeseen spin to the ceremony. Or say you want to make food like you see on television, but it turns out it's a lot harder than it looks. Your food ends up looking like it's on the Netflix show *Nailed It!* which proudly displays failed attempts at gourmet cuisine. Also, none of those shows ever reveal the stack of dishes that must be washed after such an undertaking!

Or say you want to travel. We've all seen those travel photos on Instagram in which someone is in some exotic land, all by themselves with no crowds, finding themselves, having the adventure of a lifetime, usually wearing a fedora, and you're like, *I want to go on an adventure. I want to find myself. I want to own a fedora.* So you save up your money for a year, book your tickets, and travel seventeen hours by plane, train, and bus to arrive at your destination, only to find it packed with tourists! Everyone else had the same idea. If you've ever traveled, you know the reality of travel is that it is never as it is portrayed in curated media.

It Doesn't Work

What's happening is that we try to take this curated reality we see on Pinterest, Facebook, and Instagram and apply it to our very messy, smelly, crowded, noisy, sweaty reality—and it doesn't work. It doesn't work. And day after day after day we experience the "it doesn't work" conclusion through our screens. We look at the curated photos of someone else's life and then look at our own normal and humble life and conclude, "It doesn't work." We look at someone else's manicured fashionable home, and then look at our laundry-strewn floors and no-art-on-the walls home and conclude, "It doesn't work." We look at someone's finished marathon picture while holding our middle-aged soft and bloated tummy and whisper, "It doesn't work."

We've been doing this for years—so long, in fact, that a recent study conducted by the University of Pittsburgh School of Medicine showed that heavy social media usage can cause depression: "Exposure to highly idealized representations of peers on social media elicits feelings of envy and the distorted belief that others lead happier, more successful lives."[1]

As we're scrolling through the best curated scenes from someone else's life on these platforms, we are very aware of our present failures and insecurities, and we conclude it doesn't work.

Swipe to the next.

It doesn't work.

Swipe.

It doesn't work for me.

Swipe.

It doesn't work *because of me.*

We've been doing "it doesn't work" for so long that our conclusion is *we will not find real success by actually being ourselves.* We need to be something else to find the success we want.

And when we've come to the conclusion that we can't actually find any success in our lives by being ourselves, we've entered into a deeply sacred conversation.

In fact, all faith traditions have this conversation within their historical narratives, but I want to share a story from the tradition I grew up in that illuminates this sacred conversation.

---

1. Cited in Amit Chowdhry, "Research Links Heavy Facebook and Social Media Usage to Depression," *Forbes*, April 30, 2016, www.forbes.com/sites /amitchowdhry/2016/04/30/study-links-heavy-facebook-and-social-media -usage-to-depression/?sh=10ff968f4b53; see Liu yi Lin et al., "Association between Social Media Use and Depression among U.S. Young Adults," *Depression and Anxiety*, January 19, 2016, https://doi.org/10.1002/da.22466.

Chapter 11

A Sacred Conversation

This is a line drawing cover of a painting of Saint Peter and Saint John before they were saints. The original painting is titled *Peter and John Running to the Tomb*, and it was painted by the Swiss artist Eugène Burnand.[1] Peter and John's friend had died a few days earlier. Another friend told them she had gone to the tomb to care for the dead body and had found the tomb empty. They immediately went to see for themselves, and this painting depicts them running to confirm whether the news was true.

John, in the white robe, wrote a few books in the Bible. All bestsellers. Rakes in amazing royalty checks. In one of his books, he talks about his experience with Jesus. He writes the book from the standpoint of a narrator, an observer of the story, and when he writes about himself, he writes from a third-person perspective. But he does it in a weird way. If you were to write a book about your deepest spiritual experience from a third-person perspective, I'm

1. The colors of the original painting are stunning! More colors than can be printed in this book. I highly suggest you look up the original painting.

guessing you'd probably say something like your name or "that person" or "that person who was just happy to be there." That's what most normal authors would do. But that's not what John does. He doesn't write "John" or "humbled-to-be-a-part-of-anything John," but instead refers to himself as "the disciple whom Jesus loved."[2] Fairly arrogant to say that about yourself in your own book.

We'll come back to him in a second.

Peter, on the other hand ...

We don't have time for an in-depth Bible study (you're welcome), but you know some of the highlights.

He started as a fisherman and then was called to be a fisher of men. Then there's the "I'll never deny you,"

the "get behind me, Satan,"

the "you shall never wash my feet,"

the falling asleep in the garden,

the arrest,

the cutting off an ear,

the three denials,

the three rooster crows,

the crucifixion,

the resurrection,

some weird ghost stuff,

the "I'm going fishing,"

the catching nothing,

the casting nets on the other side,

the miraculous catch,

the swimming in the underwear,

the breakfast on the beach,

the "Peter, take a walk with me,"

the "Do you love me?" three times.

---

2. John 13:23.

Jesus asks Peter if he loves him three times. He's counteracting Peter's three denials from earlier. He's restoring the relationship. And if you've ever had a broken relationship because of something you messed up and that person came back to you to mend and restore that relationship, you know the way you respond in that moment is with great humility and gratitude.

You may say something like, "Hey, you know what? Thanks for this. I mean, I'm so glad you brought this up. It's seriously been eating me alive that we've had this thing between us. I'm so sorry for what I did back there. Can you forgive me? Are we good? I hope so. I want us to be good. Are we still doing this thing? I'm ready to get back to it!"

That sounds close to what a normal person would sound like. But that's not what Peter says!

And John writes about it in his book.

[Jesus said to Peter], "Follow me!"

Peter turned and saw that *the disciple whom Jesus loved* [John wrote this about himself!] was following them . . . When Peter saw him, he asked, *"Lord, what about him?"*

Jesus answered, "If I want him to remain alive until I return, what is that to you? You must follow me."[3]

Love Container

Look. It took me a long time to realize we can be a follower of "good news," whatever it is, and still be the kind of follower who is caught up in the bad news of a comparative conversation.

We can be at the gathering, know all the words of the songs, even all the hand gestures, when to stand up and sit down, but all

---

3. John 21:19–22, italics added.

the while looking around and assessing everyone at the gathering, inwardly asking, *But what about them? Do you like them more than me, God? Because their lives look amazing. And my life kind of sucks right now. And as far as I can tell, we're doing the exact same thing.*

Or we can be a follower of "good news" who responds, *Oh, I get what this is all about. I'm the one who's loved. I'm the beloved.*

See . . .

God *is* Love.

And Love wants to pour Itself into you.

But you can't receive Love if you secretly hate the person Love made you to be.

This body/life/soul is the only container you've been given to receive Love in.

And if all you're doing day after day is trying to trade out that container, then Love will always fall flat.

You, right now, are the container Love wants to pour into.

The Dancer

I ended up at a charismatic meeting once. Only once. I grew up Lutheran, so we never talked about the Holy Spirit. He was like a bad uncle who doesn't come to holidays anymore. But if you've ever been to a charismatic meeting, it's very exciting. A lot of tambourines, flag-waving, jazz hands. It's a full-on participation celebration.

I, on the other hand, wasn't doing any of that. I was sitting silently in the back row, observing the cacophony of spirituality manifested all around me. Somebody invited me to participate by offering me a tambourine, the loudest and most forgivable of all the instruments, to play. "No, thank you." *I'm fine where I am, just observing from the back row like I usually do.*

As I was looking around, I noticed a man in the dark back corner, whom I can only describe as a chubby Dwight Schrute from *The Office*, just doing pirouettes for the Lord. It was like watching travel guide Rick Steves's tryout video for *So You Think You Can Dance.* Just a chubby, middle-aged man doing moves that six-year-olds do at ballet class. It was hilarious! And I was making fun of him so hard. Not on the outside. Inwardly and silently, I was making fun of him. I'm not a monster, people.

But I couldn't stop watching him, because he wasn't a stage person. We've all seen eccentric and boisterous stage people do their curated stage people stuff. In some ways, they have to be like that to keep our attention on the stage. But it's the people free-form dancing in the dark back corner who always draw my attention, because I know they believe in what they are doing.

I watched him for a long time, and I remember moving from inward laughter, to silence, to eventually jealousy. I remember thinking in all sincerity, *How did this guy figure out how to be so comfortable in his own skin?*

Because I want to dance. I don't want to stand on the sidelines and despise those who've figured out how to dance.

Culture of Comparison

Friends, more than any other human beings in the history of the world, we exist in a massive culture of comparison. We're exposed to comparison all day long through our phones, computer/tablet screens, billboards, and magazines, and it's literally killing us.

Conversations are happening in Silicon Valley and in our governmental agencies about what we're going to do with today's technology and how we want it to function in our lives. This explosion of social networking is so new. Social media has been around only as long as a teenager. It's still maturing, and we're going to figure it out. But until we do, we need some kind of rhythm, tool, or practice to deal with this crushing culture of comparison.

I started experimenting with a specific practice that works for me, and I want to share it with you.

You're a Contribution

Whenever you find yourself in a comparative conversation...

Like feeling like a complete loser after "deathscrolling" Instagram for ten minutes.

Or seeing someone in their bathing suit and then feeling disappointed in your own swimsuit body.

Or not enjoying a musical concert because it reflects back your own failed dreams of becoming a performer.

Or seeing someone land the promotion you worked so hard to try to get.

Or being passed up on a dating app.

Or hating your house after binge-watching HGTV home renovation shows for three hours.

Or seeing someone jog when you know your knees can't handle running anymore.

Or comparing yourself to a person who shares all the same characteristics—age, height, stage of life, gender, hair color, zodiac sign, car.

Or whatever topic you choose to allow a comparative conversation to occur about...

You need to pause, take a breath, and then move from *comparison* to *contribution*.

Say it out loud if it helps. "I am a contribution. I can be a contribution today."

If comparison is believing you need to get off your path and onto someone else's path in order to achieve the success you want, then in this case, the T-Rex of Giving Up is right: you do suck; *you suck at being someone else.*

Contribution, though, is the slow, daily work of uncovering the hidden path of desire that has been put in you to walk.

Have you ever looked back on the history of your life and felt like you were walking on some kind of path? You can see some kind of transformational pattern that the journey of your life has been leading you on. But then today, that path abruptly ends. And peering into the future? "Fuhgeddaboutit."[1] The future remains a hidden mystery.

Contribution is that slow, daily work of uncovering the hidden path of desire that has been put in you to walk.

Your desire. Your bliss. It has been put in you to follow, so you make the path by walking.

You can be a contribution to that path today.

Slow Daily Work

Contribution is the short time dedicated to writing every day that eventually gives you enough confidence to write an article, a poem, a collection of stories, and to be on your way to thinking of

---

1. Must say in the voice of an imaginary Italian uncle.

yourself as a writer instead of being distracted by a tidal wave of endless streaming content that has been keeping you from pursuing that writer dream.

Contribution is painting the walls of your house, getting rid of old stuff, hanging new art, hosting weekly dinners that change the house you thought was dated instead of waiting for some HGTV home renovation crew to magically show up at your doorstep to do the work for you.

Contribution is using your body to give hugs, hold hands, kick a ball, go for a walk with loved ones instead of groaning under the pressure of trying to prepare your body for a swimsuit photo op.

Contribution is the half mile you run every other day that eventually leads to one mile, four, seven, and then a marathon instead of the analysis paralysis of thinking you need to run like you did in high school track on your first day out.

Contribution is the daily offering of the gift of yourself in the places you can instead of waiting for someone to notice your magic through the pixels on the screen of their phone.

Contribution is nurturing the daily belief that the answers to the direction of your life are within you instead of thinking you need to attend another seminar or read another book to find them. If you take time to listen, your life will tell you the life it's looking for.

Desire offers a way for us to discover the path we are to walk. We can contribute to that path today. Every day we can lay one more row of bricks by being a contribution. Everything that exists was created by the slow, daily work of contribution. A piece of art. A new house. A degree. A garden. Firmer buttocks. A friendship. A retirement fund. But contribution doesn't necessarily mean achievements or the making of products, although I believe artifacts do come from this commitment to contribute.

What You Love and Why

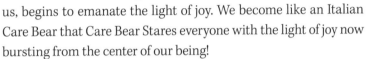

Contribution is simply our love catalyzed. It's our love set in motion. *What do I love and why?*

I love pizza (don't we all!) because pizza is a heated-up bread-sauce-and-cheese cake that, when placed inside us, begins to emanate the light of joy. We become like an Italian Care Bear that Care Bear Stares everyone with the light of joy now bursting from the center of our being!

But I also love pizza because my parents used to take my brother and me to one particular pizza joint when we were kids. It had a limited arcade, but we loved playing Teenage Mutant Ninja Turtles together while our parents ate starter salads. When the pizza was ready, or when we ran out of the spare change our parents had given us to play video games, we would sit at a booth and eat together as a family. Eating pizza reminds me that I come from a family that loves me.

What do you love and why?

A friend of mine told me about a women's shelter near her that does a group exercise with their guests. They ask the women to list anything they want in life. Anything! A no-holds-barred kind of list making. They encourage them to be really, really honest about what they want, and there are no wrong answers. These are, of course, women who have been methodically made to feel very small and unworthy over a long time, so it's an uncomfortable exercise at first. But they get into it, and the lists always hold very beautiful things. Then the shelter leaders direct them to look at their list and see for themselves: *what you love is who you are.*

And look! You love some very beautiful things.

You are very beautiful.

What do you love and why?

Love is a powerful engine. A divine engine really. And our "why" is fuel that keeps that engine humming.

Our "why" can never be a goal, an accomplishment, or a product, because those benchmarks will come and go throughout our lives. Our "why" flows from that path of our deepest desire that has been put in us to walk.

The goal of writing is less about constructing a book and more about practicing the art of imagination and mining the wisdom from our lives.

The accomplishment of exercise is less about being ready for photographs and more about enjoying the gift of our bodies.

The product of marriage is less about the number of years we chalk up together and more about the lifetime commitment to transformation through loving someone else.

What do you love and why?

We have a word for "what you love and why" in our culture, and that word is *gratitude*.

Therapists and psychologists say that writing down three instances of "what we love and why" every day, say, in a gratitude journal, can dramatically improve our mental health, our physical health, and our sleeping habits.

Gratitude can also do something else. When we write down our "what we love and whys," we're making a library of our loves. We're creating a catalogue of our loves.

CATALOGUE of LOVES

So when the Kanye West of your life comes to you with a comparative narrative and says, "Do you want to trade lives with me?" and you feel that deep temptation to say, "I don't know,

Kanye—even with all the complications, it still looks kinda cool being an internationally acclaimed rap star," you'd have to trade all of your loves in order to get that life. You'd have to set fire to your catalogue of loves for a comparison that will never be the way you thought it would be.

But if you collect enough of your loves and you're aware of this massive catalogue of loves, you'll see this acquired treasure and say, "No, Kanye! I don't want to trade lives with you. I can see all I have been given. And I've been given so much!"

Chapter 13

Catalogue of Loves

I love the song "Set Adrift on Memory Bliss" by P.M. Dawn. I love it because it reminds me of my junior high crush Lynn Voorhees, which never amounted to anything. But I love the feeling. Because to love someone or something deeply is the best feeling of all. Because to love is to desire, and to desire is to want to be here. This song reminds me of what a joy it is to be here.

My favorite smell is low tide. I love low tide. I grew up in a small Pacific Northwest town called Mukilteo, and the smell of salt and decay was always around. Low tide is magical because it reveals a world that's mostly hidden. And to walk around the tide pools and scattered kelp beds and witness that hidden world is to remember that what we see is not all there is.

I love rolled-up socks.

I love plastic sandwich bags, with or without sandwiches in them.

I love a good rainstorm.

I love the way my body feels after a long swim.

I love my body. Well, I'm trying to. I mean, I've been pro-grammed to see it as not good enough for so long, mostly in Speedo situations, that I forget what a joy it is to be incarnate in such a magical biological masterpiece. I remember this most when I hug my kids.

I love remembering that moment when my daughter was a baby, and I was lying on the bed with her. I heard the voice of God tell me she was going to be a gift to the world—and when God tells you a secret, you never forget it.

I love church. Not necessarily what we've made it in America. There's a lot of fluff that can go away as far as I'm concerned. But here's what I love. I love what happens to my eyes and my ears and my heart when I'm in the midst of a gathering. The poet Rumi has a poem that says, "Where am I going on this glorious journey? To your house, of course."[1] I believe this poem the most when we gather in Its holy name.

I love you, Giver of existence—even though I have some deep questions about your invisibility and the suffering in this world and the absurdity of salmon migrations! I see that you have given us the gift of *existing*. Admittedly, existing is trying at times. There's so much loss. Don't get me wrong. There's a lot of loss. But what a gift to receive, and what a world to live in, and what a cup to drink deeply from.

So thank you for my life. This one. With its dad tummy and its forty-year-old creaky knees and its proclivity to melancholiness (Enneagram 4!). I'm glad to be alive! I love being *here*.

We as your people want to dance in your presence, in the presence of the Giver of existence, in the presence of Existence itself.

So come, come and dance with me. Not because it's a religious thing to do, but because it's something lovers can't be stopped from doing.

---

1. Quoted in Daniel Ladinsky, *Love Poems from God: Twelve Sacred Voices from the East and West* (New York: Penguin, 2002), 60.

Chapter 14

The Dance Circle of Life

Come, come and dance with me.

Easier said than done, right? Because there's nothing more gloriously vulnerable than a dance circle. Any wedding reception, high school prom, or community park production of *Fiddler on the Roof* has a moment when the crowd forms a circle and invites anyone and everyone to publicly bust a move. It obviously starts off with the extroverts, who either display their tried-and-true best moves they've been practicing on TikTok for months or just make it up as they go, relying solely on their bravado. You'll get a couple or two who do a fun kind of choreographed duet. And every now and then, you'll get an introvert who takes the giant leap of public scrutiny as they let the music take over their body. It's a glorious witness to the human spirit.

The dancing in the middle of the circle is obviously the main event, but something interesting is happening with the people who form the circle as well. The dance circle is the launch point of contribution, and every single person forming the circle has thoughts like these: *What can I do? Do I know any dance moves? I'm not prepared for this situation. Who am I to dance in the middle? Who am I to contribute? I'll totally fail and look like an idiot if I go and dance.*

Because deep down inside we want to dance. We want to be comfortable in our own skin, busting a move without a care in the world. *We want to be a contribution.* We don't want to stand to the side and watch those who know how to dance. We want to join them! But how? How do we get past all of our feelings of inadequacy in being a contribution? All of these feelings and questions point to a phenomenon we commonly call imposter syndrome.

Imposter Syndrome

Imposter syndrome is the feeling that we shouldn't be in whatever moment we find ourselves in. It's a cocktail party of feelings of inadequacy that persist, despite the evidence that we are in some ways successful already, and the special cocktail we drink at this party is a mix of self-doubt, intellectual fraudulence, and the secret homemade ingredient of unreachable perfectionism. That's right, perfectionism. Imposter syndrome isn't based on a lack of confidence or low self-esteem. It's rooted in the idea that whatever we do, we won't do it perfectly. It will always be lacking. That we aren't qualified enough, and we'll soon be discovered to be a fraud.

Imposter syndrome is best identified in persistent thoughts or feelings that say:

> "I must not fail," because to fail proves the accusation that you're a failure. That you don't have what it takes to be successful by being you.

"I feel like a fake," because deep down you feel like you're unworthy of success.

"It's all up to luck," because real success doesn't come from persistent dedication to a goal or an achievement; success comes to those who are blessed by fate (I see you, Carl Jung "you will call it fate" quote callback).

A few years ago, I was hired by a design agency in Portland, Oregon. It was my first time working at an agency like this, and even though the leaders of this agency sought me out, the experience felt intimidating. The office was super swanky, complete with a full coffee and snack bar that became an appetizer and drinks bar in the afternoon. The place was decked out with rad furniture, mod art, and killer workspaces. Everyone I worked with was so cool—like edgy, Portland-hipster cool. It was like going to work with The Flaming Lips and I was Smash Mouth. But I became friends with my coworkers, got used to the space, and learned how to make gourmet pour-overs for our visiting clients.

I remember talking to one of my bosses one afternoon and vulnerably admitting that I felt intimidated as I came to work each day. He tilted his head as a grin appeared on his cooler-than-cool hipster face. "Dude. Everyone feels the same way. I do. My bosses do. Your coworkers do. Everyone is just making it up as they go."

Everyone is just making it up as they go. From my perspective, no truer words have ever been spoken. Everyone, no matter how successful, has these feelings from time to time.

This notion was corroborated in an interview on the podcast *How I Built This.*[1] Host Guy Raz interviewed YouTube sensation,

---

1. "Video Artist: Casey Neistat," interview by Guy Raz, *How I Built This* podcast

electric skateboarding guru, and possible superhero Casey Neistat, whose daily vlogging and low-fi filming style have shaped much of what vlogging looks like today. The interview is great, and they talk about all of Casey's successes that have led to his being a multimillionaire. Unexpectedly, Casey mentions that earlier in the morning, before he and Guy talked together, Casey met with his therapist and discussed his imposter syndrome feelings. *Excuse me? I beg your pardon? You, Casey Neistat, with double-digit-million YouTube subscribers, still have feelings of being an imposter?* Yes. And of course he can, because these feelings aren't resolved by achievement or success; they are only reduced by practicing empathy and reframing the narrative.

Practicing Empathy

You've spent most of your life with your own feelings, which would make sense because you are you and you live in your body. All of us tend to spend most of our time thinking about ourselves. We spend hardly any time thinking about what it would be like to be in someone else's head, heart, feelings, and body. One of the ways to curb the feelings of imposter syndrome is to *empathize* with everyone around us and realize they have similar feelings as they live in their own bodies. The lie of imposter syndrome is that we are the only ones who feel inadequate, insecure, incapable, afraid, and boring, with nothing to offer. But the truth is that everyone around us has feelings of inadequacy, feelings of not being prepared, feelings of not having what it takes, like they're making it up as they go.

(with Guy Raz), March 2, 2020, www.npr.org/2020/02/28/810412631/video-artist
-casey-neistat.

It's almost like the better I do, the more my feeling of inadequacy actually increases, because I'm just going, *Any moment, someone's going to find out I'm a total fraud, and that I don't deserve any of what I've achieved. I can't possibly live up to what everyone thinks I am and what everyone's expectations are of me.*

Emma Watson, actor and activist[2]

Very few people, whether you've been in that job before or not, get into the seat and believe today that they are now qualified to be the CEO. They're not going to tell you that, but it's true.

Howard Schultz, CEO of Starbucks[3]

No matter what we've done, there comes a point where you think, "How did I get here? When are they going to discover that I am, in fact, a fraud and take everything away from me?"

Tom Hanks, director and actor[4]

Who doesn't suffer from imposter syndrome? Even when I sold my business for $66 Million, I felt like an absolute fraud!

Barbara Corcoran, real estate
agent and *Shark Tank* judge[5]

---

2. Quoted in Tavi Gevinson, "I Want It to Be Worth It: An Interview with Emma Watson," *Rookie* magazine, May 27, 2013, www.rookiemag.com/2013/05/emma-watson-interview/2.
3. Quoted in Adam Bryant, "Good C.E.O.'s Are Insecure (and Know It)," *New York Times*, October 9, 2010.
4. "Tom Hanks Says Self-Doubt Is 'A High-Wire Act That We All Walk,'" *Fresh Air* podcast, April 26, 2016, www.npr.org/2016/04/26/475573489/tom-hanks-says-self-doubt-is-a-high-wire-act-that-we-all-walk.
5. Barbara Corcoran, Twitter post, February 25, 2020, https://twitter.com/barbaracorcoran/status/1232486330904399876.

You will never climb Career Mountain and get to the top and shout, "I made it!" You will rarely feel done or complete or even successful. Most people I know struggle with that complicated soup of feeling slighted on one hand and a total fraud on the other.

Amy Poehler, comedian[6]

I have written eleven books, but each time I think, "Uh-oh, they're going to find out now. I've run a game on everybody, and they're going to find me out."

Maya Angelou, poet[7]

What people really think of me is something I remain blissfully unaware of most of the time. I love acting and all I ever try to do is my best. But even now I always dread those emotional scenes. I'm there thinking, "Oh my God, I'm rubbish and everyone is going to see it. They've cast the wrong person." But I have come to realise that those nerves are all part of the process for me . . . Sometimes I wake up in the morning before going off to a shoot, and I think, "I can't do this. I'm a fraud."

Kate Winslet, actor[8]

Unless they say it into a microphone, we may never know how many musicians we've seen play publicly have been racked with nerves about not being good enough onstage. We may never know that the person running the marathon is having an internal

---

6. Amy Poehler, *Yes Please* (New York: Dey Street, 2014), 225.
7. Quoted in Margie Warrell, "Afraid of Being 'Found Out'? How to Overcome Impostor Syndrome," *Forbes*, April 3, 2014, www.forbes.com/sites/margiewarrell /2014/04/03/impostor-syndrome.
8. Quoted in "Kate Winslet: 'I Still Worry I'm a Rubbish Actor,'" *The Mirror*, February 22, 2009, www.mirror.co.uk/3am/celebrity-news/kate-winslet-i-still-worry-377360.

conversation about not having what it takes to finish the race. We may never know the secret insecure conversations someone has in their bedroom as they change into their work clothes for the day ahead. Every painting I've ever made is an emotional roller coaster of excitement, self-doubt, horror, failure, acceptance, and surprise. No wonder artists are a bit kooky. The creative process is an excavator of all kinds of hidden doubts, fears, and uncertainties.

But through this process of being with your feelings, you become the kind of person who can move forward with them instead of being hindered by them. *Imposter syndrome is really just being a stranger to your feelings.* The lie is that walking the secret path of desire put in you to walk is going to be a journey without complicated feelings. We assume that when we reach some desired destination, we will finally be free of these feelings of inadequacy. So when we start to contribute in the way we can, we dismiss ourselves when we feel these feelings, but in fact, we could say we're on the right path because of these feelings. So let's give grace to ourselves and accept that we have complicated feelings. Everyone does.

Reframing the Narrative

Anyone who endeavors to pursue anything is learning as they go. *I'm on my way* means I want to keep learning. It's completely normal not to know everything throughout our lives. In fact, it would be completely odd to think we should know everything. That's why college freshmen who've taken one philosophy or religion class are so annoying. The process of learning happens as we progress on our journey. We learn as we go forward, not by staying put.

But, yes, learning can look awkward. Have you ever seen

someone learning to ice-skate for the first time? And not just a child but a fully formed, competent adult human being? No one starts off ice-skating like a pro. Most everyone starts off with petite, self-conscious steps while holding the ice rink wall with wide-eyed concentration, knowing at any moment their legs could shoot out from underneath them, crashing their denim-wearing behind onto the unforgiving ice floor. Nothing is more awkward and cringeworthy than watching sophisticated *Homo sapiens*, capable of putting their own species on the moon, just mercilessly landing on their backsides as they learn to ice-skate. It's a ubiquitous sight at the local ice rink because learning to ice-skate is really hard. And it takes time. Yet it's so fun when we start to get the hang of it.

When we're stuck in a comparative conversation or feeling like we're about to be discovered as a complete fraud, it helps to imagine the person we're comparing ourselves with—our hero, the expert in our field, someone we look up to, someone we hope to be like one day—learning to ice-skate for the first time. Imagine them taking to the ice for the first time in their life. I guarantee they won't look awesome. Even if it's Kanye West, he'll still look vulnerable taking those baby steps in his custom futuristic ice skates as he hugs the rink wall, just like you and I feel right now with what we're trying to do. Because we're learning. And it feels vulnerable to try. And we don't feel smooth and confident but kind of awkward and about to fall on our denim-clad buttocks. And that's exactly how everyone feels who decides to be a contribution.

So say it. "I'm a contribution. I can be a contribution today."

For me, I found there are three avenues that I keep in mind

when I claim I can be a contribution today. I believe contribution happens through *gratitude*, *convergence*, and *being a conduit*.

Gratitude as Contribution

Earlier, I mentioned the practice of writing in a gratitude journal and even provided in chapter 13 a small sample of what that could be like. A gratitude journal is simply a landing place for our thoughts and feelings of gratitude. It is not gratitude itself. That is something secret—something hidden and within.

Maybe you already have a gratitude journal practice, like I do, but let's pretend you don't. To start, you would acquire a bound notebook and write "Gratitude Journal" on the front. You'd grab your favorite pen and start writing down everything you are grateful for. A beautiful song. Good health. Loving companions in life. The way the sun reflects off the water at sunset. The heavenly taste of cookie dough. And so on and so forth. Maybe you're someone who could list a million things. Maybe you're more of a quality-versus-quantity kind of person. Maybe you're one who after forty-seven gratitude entries doesn't know what else to write down. Even the one who can write a million things will eventually run out of things to write. So what do you do then? And the bigger question then is, *Is writing down everything you're grateful for even the point?*

Often we unconsciously write down what we think will sound cool, poetic, or meaningful if these listed items were to be read by someone else. Granted, that was the point of what I wrote down in my "catalogue of loves" section earlier. I recite that list out loud in my live performance in front of an audience, so when

I wrote it, I was aiming to evoke a deep, heartfelt experience. As I shared it in this book, I hoped it would do the same thing. But if I were to write it for myself, would I have written it that way? Maybe not, although I will say the practice of framing your daily life in a poetic form can be deeply meaningful. My point is that our gratitude journal is not for others to see, but the exercise is meant to lead us to rest in a state of gratitude.

Do we have to invent stuff to be grateful for? Is that the point of this exercise? No! The point of writing in a gratitude journal is to help us move to a *state of gratitude*.

When we take the time to reflect on, name, and catalogue our loves, we're reminded that we've been given a lot of goodness in our lives. That there are elements of our lives that make life worth living. We receive the gift of life and want to say yes to it. And we notice that some of the sources of this goodness are found outside ourselves. We can be grateful for other people, landscapes, animals—to the entire world and beyond. We can observe the goodness of our lives and who to thank for it. Being in a state of gratitude is saying yes to the intertwined life we find ourselves in.

State of Gratitude

I've found a way to live in the world that is pure magic, and it's based on a prayer I have hanging up in my studio:

> *You will be given everything you need to accomplish*
> *what you have been asked to do.*

For one, it believes in abundance versus scarcity. Second, it acknowledges that I'm on my way. That I have a path of desire that has been put in me to walk and that I'm not pursuing this path solely on my own. Providence is working behind the scenes in surprising and unexpected ways. And finally, it invites me to find everything I need hidden in the life I'm living right now. This is what a state of gratitude reveals: *you have everything you need right now.*

This abundant way of living was cleverly portrayed in the television show *MacGyver.* Remember this show? Not only did the lead actor, Richard Dean Anderson, have a killer mullet, but he had the coolest job too. He worked for a company called the Phoenix Foundation, which did who knows what. From what I remember, they never really explained their purpose, but MacGyver's job was basically to be a situational problem solver. In every episode, Mac found himself in some seemingly impossible situation. But with his knowledge of chemistry, physics, and good old-fashioned handyman know-how, he would find everything he needed in unexpected places to get him out of a jam—mostly with the creative use of duct tape and some bleach cleaner sitting on a shelf. It was a fun show, for sure, but I think it spoke to the profound truth that what we need to accomplish, what we want to do, is already in our midst.

I once did a performance in downtown Los Angeles on a Sunday at ten in the morning. I had flown in late the night before and had sent a list of materials I needed to the venue host in advance because I knew no stores would be open late Saturday night or early Sunday. One of the items I needed most was a large framed canvas. This particular performance involved a piece of art that would be created during the show and then become the focal piece at the end of the performance. I got to the venue early in the morning and began setting up all my tech and stage pieces. I also had to set up my own merch table. Thirty minutes before the performance was about to start, I asked the venue host where the canvas he had acquired was hiding. He looked at me wide-eyed, like I had just asked him to recite the names of all the Kardashians. "I totally forgot to get one. I'm so sorry."

I was in downtown LA. No art stores are open at nine thirty in the morning! And the building had no art supplies that I could use instead of a canvas. But I had been in this place before, and I stopped and whispered, *You will be given everything you need to accomplish what you've been asked to do.*

I sat in this state for a moment, and I thought to ask, "Do you have any kind of attic or basement where you keep a lot of stuff?" He told me they did indeed, so we hurried down the stairs and entered an immense basement. *Ah, surely they'll have something in here*, I thought. But as we walked through the whole area, I saw nothing. Defeated, I began to go up the stairs when I noticed something hidden behind the door. It was the kind of kitschy art piece you might find on sale at a thrift store. But this canvas was wrapped on a wooden frame. I didn't have any paint to cover up the hideous painting, but I turned the frame over to discover that nothing had been painted on the back side. It was workable! "Can I use this?" I asked. "Absolutely," he said. "That's been lying around down here for years."

Many things may have been lying around for years—things we've never noticed before—that might provide a solution to a problem we're facing. Maybe stuff in a basement. But maybe also friends, relationships, experiences, perspectives, loves, and abilities. Things you've easily overlooked day by day. You never know where what you need in this situation is hiding in the reality around you. Living in a state of gratitude helps give you the eyes to reveal these hidden solutions.

Convergence as Contribution

I once was the second cameraman on a documentary being filmed in Swaziland. At the time, I was facilitating a humanitarian art project with another nonprofit when I got the call from a friend of mine who was producing a movie in Swaziland at the same time, saying they had to fire their second cameraman and they were wondering if I wanted to extend my trip and finish the shoot with them. "Obviously, the answer is yes!" I responded.

It was a small-budget film, and the lead cameraman I was working alongside was also the director of the film. His name is Helmut Schleppi, which is fantastically Dutch. A fun fact about Helmut is that he has visited every country in the world, and even Antarctica twice, because he worked on a European travel show for seven years. Amazing!

One night we were chatting about how the film industry has evolved over the years, and what he shared can help us understand how we can be a unique contribution to the world. He said that in the early 1980s, you could know how to do one thing in film production and make a decent living. But that has changed. Today, one must know how to do many different things in terms of filmmaking to build a career out of it. For this film alone, not only was he the director and main cameraman, but he was going to be the editor and a partial producer as well. That's just how the industry has changed.

You may have heard grandiose tales of ancient artists who studied for thirty years to perfect one brushstroke while you lament that you haven't had a single job lasting longer than three years. We live in a complex world, and today more than ever we need to know a lot of different things to make any kind of career happen. We may know how to fashion the most beautiful canoes the world has ever seen, but unless we also know how to create a website and have a snazzy social media strategy, the world may never know about our canoes. We have to know a lot, and because we know a lot, we may have a sense we don't know anything really deeply at all. We may feel like we'll never become the master of anything but are doomed to be a master of nothing.

But this notion is, in fact, not true. We just need to change what we think we're becoming a master of.

Let's take the idea of a dance circle, but instead of the circle consisting of individual people, let's imagine the circle is comprised of what we love, identified by our gratitude practice.

The dancer in the middle is not one thing but the convergence of what we love. We do not become the master of each individual love we have. What we become a master of is the way these loves uniquely come together in us and in our contribution. We are the master of this convergence.

What Are You Looking For?

I remember lamenting to my painter friend Jeremy that every time I looked at art in local galleries and openings, I couldn't find anything I really liked. I hadn't seen anything that inspired me. He responded, "The problem isn't the art you're looking at; the problem is you're not finding the art you know you want to be making. You should be making what you're trying to find."

I got a clearer understanding of what he meant when my wife

and I visited some friends in Philadelphia. While there, we visited the Philadelphia Museum of Art, which you might remember not for its art collection but for the steps that fictional boxer Rocky Balboa ran up and celebrated on in the classic scene from the movie bearing his name. But the museum does have an amazing collection! Super-famous stuff I studied in college, like Marcel Duchamp's *Nude Descending a Staircase, No. 2*, which I'm sure you're familiar with. (Art school joke.) It's a great museum, and it cost us $35 apiece to enter—and being the poor creatives we were, we were determined to get as much out of it as we could. After about three hours though, I was losing my fervor at merely looking at art hanging on a wall. I wanted more. I thought, *This is amazing stuff, but it's still not as cool as a rock show.* I wanted more interaction. For example, they were hosting a wonderful exhibit of a visiting collection of Edgar Degas paintings. They were all professionally hung and presented just like you expect to see great art displayed, but I was hoping for more. If I'd had my druthers, I would have loved to have some actor or a hologram pretending to be Degas with an exaggerated French accent meet me at the entrance and welcome me to look at his art with him.

"Ziz iz Chloë, my neighb-hor, who let me paint hare portrait one day."

"Ziz iz zee backyard of my friend François. J'adore I love how zee light— mmm, how do you say?—glowz off zee flowerz at zunzet."

"Ziz iz zee café where I zit wit my frondz and have a café au lait and dizcuzz what we are working on."

I wanted the artist to walk with me and show me where his

art came from. How the art pieces were, in fact, the artifacts of a human life lived in this world. To be clear, this should not be the expectation of all artists and their art. But this was a revealing moment for me about the work I should be doing.

What is it you want to do?

And what do you love?

And who are you? And where have you come from?

These are all the elements that will come together, that *will converge*, in your unique way of contribution. Everything has been done and said already. And yet new artifacts of human lives emerge every day. New businesses. New art. New classes. New adventures. Why? Because the ingredient of *you* changes all of these contributions.

If we think about it, creativity is essentially the juxtaposition of unexpected elements. That's why when we see something we haven't seen before, we say, "That's so creative." Take some drumbeats and a sample of an old gospel song, juxtapose them with modern street poetry, and you get rap. Add some Southern flare to it, and you get the group OutKast. Take tire repair, juxtapose employees running upon your arrival, and you have Les Schwab Tire Centers. Save parts of an old house, juxtapose them with new modern materials, and you've described all the best interior designers on Instagram. Take passenger jet travel, juxtapose it with retired theater kids, and you get the entire Southwest Airlines flight attendant crew.

We can always juxtapose an unexpected element with anything that has already been said and done, and our makeup constitutes that unexpected element. Our thoughts, feelings, insights, perspectives, likes, loves, dislikes, history, families, environment, geography, voice, body, biology, preferences, fears, and dreams are what uniquely shape our contribution.

"I am the contribution."

Find Your Expanders

One of the ways we can discover our convergence of loves that leads to a unique contribution is by paying attention to who expands possibilities for us. An "expander" is an individual who helps enlarge the possibility of what a human life can look like. When we see what they're doing and how they're doing it, the walls of possibility enlarge for us because they've shown us that this kind of expression is possible in the world.

The first recorded person to break the four-minute mile was a British twenty-five-year-old medical student named Roger Bannister. For years, so many athletes had tried and failed to run a mile in less than four minutes that it was commonly believed to be humanly impossible. But on a less than ideal weather day in 1954, Bannister crossed the finish line at 3 minutes, 59.4 seconds. As soon as the first part of his time was announced—"three minutes"—the watching crowd lost their minds in celebration! But his world record did not last long. Subsequent runners repeatedly lowered the time with a mix of controlled-climate conditions and improvement in running techniques. *Once it became a possibility for one person, it became a possibility for many more.*

This happens all the time around us. We know about all the big perspective changes, such as cell phones, alternative fuels, and Mars exploration that expand our horizons. But we may not have paid attention to how simple decisions by individuals can change our whole perspective on how one can live a life.

A mom decides to start writing a blog about her thoughts and feelings as a woman in the midst of transformation, and thousands, if not millions, find solidarity in her confessions. A young family decides to buck the pressure to buy a house and instead buys an old RV and engages in an alternative pattern of living a life together on the road. A young man uses his college money to buy expensive music software to pursue his deepest dream of being a composer. Someone takes a gap year to reset the way they've been doing everything and comes back with wisdom and insight that change their community. All of these decisions were made by listening to one's deepest desires and then asking how to adjust their life to pursue those desires. *Their pursuit gives us permission to pursue our desires as well.*

It may not be just one person who expands our possibilities, but different individuals who expand different parts of us. We can use the dance circle image again as a metaphor for the way that different individuals help us in our unique contributions.

Around the circle are different individuals who expand different parts of us, with the convergence of these possibilities manifest in us in the middle.

Vocationally, there isn't just one person I hope to emulate in my creative work, but I've gathered a great cloud of expanders who point me to my own unique contribution. The comedian Mike Birbiglia expands in me the possibility of telling funny but deeply human stories in a long-form format. The preacher Nadia Bolz-Weber expands in me the possibility of communicating sacredly and personally in just under ten minutes. Thomas Kinkade (yes, the "Painter of Light") expands in me the possibility of scaling a successful business of selling art. The poet David Whyte expands in me the possibility of excavating and offering deep wisdom through the fabrication of art. The comedian Hannah Gadsby expands in me the possibility of talking about whatever I want to talk about and finding an audience grateful for my insight. Vincent van Gogh expands in me the truth that selling only one painting throughout a person's lifetime doesn't mean it wasn't a valuable journey.

Whose life and work open you up to delightful possibility? Who expands you? What are the ingredients of their life that speak most deeply to you? Why? What are they doing that you hope to do? As my painter friend Jeremy told me, *whatever we're looking for is the work we should be doing.*

Being a Conduit as Contribution

What do I mean when I say *being a conduit*?

Isn't it interesting that the main hurdle of imposter syndrome is a question not of capability but of identity? "Who am I to . . .?" seems to be the first words of every statement when dismissing ourselves from pursuing our deepest longing. The conversation immediately turns to feeling like a fraud—feeling unworthy to be the medium through which this offering would come. So who are we?

There are countless ways to talk about identity and worthiness, and with such infinite options, I think the best way to talk about this is just to get really personal.

My Weird and Awesome Mystical Experience

A number of years before my toilet incident, I experienced a full-on career burnout. Later my therapist would say I began a long depressive season initiated by a moment of burnout. That moment occurred while I was sitting at a long table with my coworkers. I was on my laptop, doing whatever I was doing that day, when I heard an inaudible sound of breaking glass and everything that was holding me together seemed to fall apart. I immediately began to cry, and Paul, one of my coworkers sitting next to me, asked, "Hey, are you okay?" I responded through tears, "I don't know. I don't know what's happening to me. I'm just really tired. And I actually don't know why I get up in the morning anymore."

In addition to beginning therapy, I started to meet with an older woman in my church named Rosemary, who would pray with me. She had come alongside some friends of mine during a hard season of their lives, and they said it had really helped them. To be clear, when I met with Rosemary, I had nothing to offer. She would just speak words of wisdom or sit with me in silence at a time when I had no strength to muster any kind of spiritual practice. The musician Nick Cave writes, "[Prayer] asks us to present ourselves to the unknown as we are, devoid of pretense and affectation, and to contemplate exactly what it is we love or cherish. Through this conversation with our inner self we confront the nature of our own existence."[9] This is a big ask! And sometimes it's invaluable to have an advocate while presenting ourselves to the unknown.

During our fourth time meeting together, Rosemary said she was going to do something called Theophostic prayer. "It's a big word! But simply, *theo* means 'God' and *phostic* means 'light,' so we're just going to ask God to bring light to your situation." We met in my art studio, and Rosemary sat on a chair while I found a comfortable seat on the couch next to her. She began to pray.

A couple of odd things began to happen. One, as Rosemary was praying, my eyelids began to feel like they had sandbags attached to them. I tried to keep them open, but I was beginning

9. Quoted in Nick Reilly, "Nick Cave Reflects on Prayer and Religion in New Message: 'A Prayer to Who?'" *NME*, April 17, 2020, www.nme.com/news /music/nick-cave-reflects-on-prayer-and-religion-in-new-message-a-prayer -to-who-2648905.

to feel like I would two hours after our Thanksgiving feast when the digesting turkey would call me into dreamland. I wasn't sleepy, but I couldn't keep my eyes open. I eventually relented and let my eyelids close.

The second thing that happened is that in some mysterious way, I began to sink down into myself. When we talk about our bodies, we are referencing a couple of bodies. There's all this biological fantasticness we call our physical body. But there's another body we can't quite put a finger on. We sometimes call it our soul, our consciousness, our spirit. It's the invisible self, enmeshed in our visible self, that we know to be the truer part of us. If I were to point to that part of me, often it would feel like it's up in my head, and as I closed my eyes, I could feel that part of me slowly move down into my gut. It seemed to become really small and compact too, like I could almost feel my hollowed-out head and torso come together right in the center of me.

As I sat in this space, I began to see a scene in my mind's eye. It appeared blurry at first. Like looking at something in a fog, the closer I got to the scene, the clearer it became. I saw some green and blue. Then some trees and a grassy field and a baseball diamond and then a bunch of people. As I looked around, I realized I was in a scene from elementary school. I told Rosemary and explained the backstory of this moment.

When I was in the sixth grade, at the end of the year someone devised a rite of passage for all the elementary school grades that looked like a softball match between the teachers and the students. Now, there were just enough teachers as positions in the game, but there were way more students than positions available for a student team. We knew there would be a selection process based on who was deemed the coolest in our class. At the time, I didn't know what made you cool or not cool; I just knew I wasn't in the cool category. What I did know is that from a very young age, I had been training for this moment, because I had been involved with Little League baseball since I was five years old. In my mind, even though I wasn't cool, I was still uniquely skilled to offer help to my prepubescent classmates—and this was my moment to do so.

The moment for choosing teams came, and I didn't get picked. I was devastated. More than devastated; I was mad. I was mad because I knew I had something to offer, and no one else could see it. I wanted to be in the game so bad that I figured out a loophole for how I could participate. I made myself a base coach, which is a really important position in a game between adults and children.

So on this field in Mukilteo, Washington, in the Pacific Northwest region of the United States, the game commenced. I wanted to be in the game so bad that I never left the field. That's right—I was a base coach for the enemy as well. In one particular inning, I was just off the third base line when a teacher hit a pop fly foul ball that came right toward me. Being trained in the art of Little League, I immediately ran for it. I didn't have a glove or a hat because I wasn't really even in the game, but when I saw that ball come toward me, I instinctually ran toward it. As this large, spinning orb made its way to the earth, I gleefully jumped to meet it, excited to be a part of the game. But the spinning softball was too much for my tiny gloveless hands, and it bounced off and fell to the ground. I remember feeling disappointed I had dropped the ball when I became aware of the yelling.

"What are you doing?"

"Get off the field!"

"That could have been an out. You're not even in the game!"

All of my classmates were yelling at me, rightly so, because I wasn't in the game and that could've been the third and final out. I was completely embarrassed, as all of us would be at that age, and I made my way off the field to join the rest of the students looking on from the bleachers. As the game recommenced,

I moved to the back of the crowd. The game kept going, and without anyone noticing, I slowly disappeared from the crowd and made my way back to my desk and sat there until the school day ended. I remember realizing for the first time as I sat there alone, *This is what it must feel like when you don't belong.*

In this vision I was having, I was on the field right when I dropped the ball. Everything was in a kind of slow-motion loop. My teachers were there. My classmates were there shouting in slow mo, "Geeeeeeeeettttt ooooooooofffffffff." And I was there with my sixth-grade self. It's very hard to explain, but we weren't different people. We were just different time stamps of each other. Like he could see out of my eyes, and I could see out of his. It was a very peculiar moment.

With my eyes closed, I explained all this to Rosemary and added that I thought this was a bizarre moment to be brought to. I mean, I hadn't thought about this moment in years, and it seemed a little random, considering the seriousness of where I was finding myself presently. She responded that she understood how I felt but wanted to honor the fact that this was the moment I was led to. "So let's ask that light would be brought to this situation. *Jesus, would you bring light to this situation?*"

Then this Jesus appeared in the situation. You know the one—white robe, gold sash, blond hair, cousin of the god Thor—the Jesus from the Sunday school comics I had grown up with. I instinctively knew it was a fake Jesus, and I described to Rosemary what I was seeing. "Rosemary, a fake Jesus showed up. Is that supposed to happen?" I asked.

"It's never happened before in my experience. But if that's the one who showed up, let's ask him. *Jesus, would you bring light to this situation?*"

Fake Jesus then looked at me and my sixth-grade self and said, "Scott, this is something that happened to you as a kid. You're an adult now. You know how to navigate this situation. You don't need to let it have so much weight in your life." I shared this response with Rosemary, and she asked me what I thought about that statement.

As I looked at the vision, nothing had changed. Everything was unfolding in the same way. "I thought if light was going to be brought to this situation, it would change things in some way. But everything has remained the same. Nothing has changed. So I'm sorry, fake Jesus. Those are nice words, but they don't do anything."

"Let's ask again," Rosemary said. *"Jesus, would you bring light to this situation?"*

And then we were no longer on the field but sitting in my classroom. It was me, fake Jesus, and my six-year-old self sitting at my desk.

Fake Jesus looked at us and said, "Scott, this is just kid emotions. This is something you felt when you were a kid. You're an adult now, and you know how to navigate this. You don't need to let it have so much weight in your life."

Again I relayed this to Rosemary, and again she asked me what I thought about this statement, and again I said pretty much the same thing. I thought if light was going to be brought to this situation, at least something would change. But nothing had changed.

I guess it's ridiculous to think that the past can be changed. As far as I know, there's no DeLorean wired with a flux capacitor to go back in time and change the events of Hill Valley. Nobody can change the past. Not even God.

"So I'm sorry, fake Jesus. It just isn't working."

Fake Jesus disappeared, and I found myself back on the softball field with my classmates and my sixth-grade self. At this point, I was feeling very skeptical that this experience would come to any resolution. "Let's ask one more time," Rosemary whispered. *"Jesus, would you bring light to this situation?"*

Now, I don't really know how to describe *Jesus* to you because I could only see him out of the corner of my eye the entire time. But the impression I got was a paradoxical meeting together of the infinite and the finite. Like the immense, unfathomable expanse of the universe juxtaposed inside a man who had long hair and a beard and wore simple, earth-toned clothing. He didn't even say anything. He just walked over to me and gave me a side hug, wrapping his arm around and over my shoulder and then plunging his hand into my torso. He then began to lift. It felt like I had on the kind of lead vest you wear when you get X-rays taken by a radiology technician or a dental hygienist—like a heavy covering. He lifted and lifted and lifted until I could see it.

Light!

Bright, blinding light. Like looking at the sun but being able to hold that gaze without my retinas burning out. The light was warm, and it was moving, and it felt like embodied peace.

It stopped everything. I gasped. My classmates gasped. We all stood there with our mouths open in a state of gasp, just looking at the light because all you want to do is keep looking at it.

Then after a couple of minutes, I heard Jesus say, "Scott, this is who you really are. This is who I made you to be."

I realized in that moment what I was seeing. In Western Catholic and Protestant traditions, we often use Latin to describe the concept of our identity: *imago Dei* . . . the image of God. The ancient Hebrew writers used "image of God" language to describe human beings. In the Bible book of Genesis—the poem describing the beginning of all things—we see a Creator who takes all the elements of the universe, or simply dirt, and makes a form out of that dirt. But what gives that form life isn't the form itself; rather it is the *breath* of the Creator that gives life. The word there is *ruach*. The Hebrew word for wind, breath, Spirit. That *ruach* is what gives the form life—the light of life. And just as my chromosomes are in my children, so is the *ruach* in me. It's not a question of whether I am or am not a child of the Creator; it's a realization that I can never stop being one. Ever.

As I was looking at the light, I inquired, "How do I not lose sight of this?" Without any pretension, he responded, "Just be with me. When you're with me, you'll always see it in yourself and you'll always see it in others." I looked up and could see the light inside my classmates. I could see the light inside my teachers. *I could see the light inside everyone in the whole world.*

I was overwhelmed by this vision. It was like the whole world had become newly illuminated. Like those images from space where the world is covered in darkness but you can see the lights of cities dotted along the landscape, except in this moment the light dotting the earth was my fellow human beings. We are all "the light of the world."[10]

Still reeling from this vision, I asked, "What do you want me to do with this?"

He said, "Whenever you speak to people, call out the light in them. Speak to the light *in* them."

And then I opened my eyes.

---

10. Matthew 5:14.

Be the Conduit

What does it mean to be a conduit?

A conduit simply means a passageway of some kind that is a thruway for whatever is needing to be delivered. We often use the word *conduit* to refer to the passage of energy from one place to another. It's how one thing ends up in another thing. The only real criteria for a conduit are that it would be open, willing, and connected.

A few years ago, I was invited to be in an intimate group of people who were privileged to sit with Franciscan friar Richard Rohr at his Center for Action and Contemplation in Albuquerque, New Mexico. Rohr is a Catholic priest and a prolific spiritual writer. PBS has called him "one of the most popular spirituality authors and speakers in the world."[11] The theme of the weekend was "Belong," with conversations about leadership, identity, gender, and harmony. It was a fantastic opportunity to be with a myriad of leaders from all over the country discussing what it means to belong to a tradition, a faith, a community, and a human body.

After one of the sessions, we had a question-and-answer time with Father Rohr in which we could ask him anything on our minds. One man raised his hand and said, "You're a prolific writer. You've written around thirty books, and you're still going. To what do you attribute your having been able to create so much?"

Father Rohr's answer is a quote I have hanging in my studio. He said, "When I realized I didn't need to be the creator of content but the *conduit of content*, things got a lot easier."

Be the conduit.

---

11. Quoted in "Richard Rohr," *PBS: Religion and Ethics Newsweekly*, November 11, 2011, www.pbs.org/wnet/religionandethics/2011/11/11/november-11-2011 -richard-rohr/9902.

The "who are you?" of imposter syndrome is imbued with the idea that you're not worthy of doing whatever it is you're doing. That you haven't earned the right to be in this moment. That you're a fraud. That you'll be exposed as a fake.

In some way, our work is trying to earn that worthiness. I'm not talking about the process of developing a skill. Those we find in exceptional places are usually the ones who have developed exceptional skills. I'm talking about the feeling that who you are is good enough.

Worthiness

What I learned from my burnout is that the engine of earning love through accomplishment is a strong engine. It will get us out of bed in the morning, but it eventually leads to self-destruction. It works for a while, but it's not sustainable. To do anything truly sustainable that doesn't lead to complete self-destruction, I had to change from working *for* identity to working *from* identity.

You can't receive love if you secretly hate who love made you to be. This you—your body, mind, soul, and spirit—this existence, is the container you've been given to receive love in. It is the container that becomes the conduit for this love to be poured out into the world.

You are the conduit for Love.

Being a conduit is nothing you have to earn. Nothing you need to be better for. Nothing others have that you don't have. Being a conduit is something your eyes become open to only when you accept the gift of yourself. The gift of your incarnation.

"Am I worthy or not?" is the wrong question. Worthiness is not something that is earned; it is something we are awakened to. Catholic monk and social activist Thomas Merton wrote, "The root of Christian love is . . . *the faith that one is loved*. The faith that one is loved *by God*. That faith that one is loved by God although *unworthy*—or, rather, irrespective of one's worth!"[12] The good news that the apostle John identified was his understanding that he was the one who was loved. He was beloved. It wasn't something he earned. It was an identity he was awakened to. Worthiness is an innate identity given to us by the Giver.

Contribute the Light

Belovedness is not our default mode. Sure, I shared with you my weird but awesome mystical experience where I saw the innate belovedness in all of humanity, but I lose sight of that on the daily. I have to practice that belovedness every day, and I can do it by being a contribution, allowing myself to be a conduit of love.

I can be a conduit of love when I hug my children and speak a kind word to them. I can be a conduit of love when I contribute a listening and empathetic ear to a friend who is hurting. I can be a conduit of love when I clean the toilets at my aging parents' house because, Lord knows, bending down to scrub that bowl can be hard on your knees. But most poignantly, I can be a conduit of love when I allow myself to be the medium that an idea, a passion, a dream, a desire, a thought, an action, a perspective, an intuition comes through. I must receive the gift of myself in order to be a clear passageway for love and light to pass through.

When people contribute, light is produced. "They lit up the room!" "Let your light shine!" When people contribute, reality is illuminated. Our hearts are awakened. Something is ignited in us. Contribution points to our own burning light.

---

12. Quoted in Thomas P. McDonnell, ed., *A Thomas Merton Reader* (New York: Image, 1974), 322, italics in original.

So let's take the dance circle illustration and tweak it a bit. The interesting thing about contribution is twofold.

Just like the dancer in the middle can inspire those around  them to dance, so can contributing our light ignite the light in others.

Also, when others contribute, the fire in us can be ignited again.

This is why our contribution is so important. We have no idea how our light may ignite someone else's light. "Well," we may say, "it's not as good as someone else's." Halt the comparison. Move to contribution. We can be a contribution today. We can be a conduit of light. It is this light we must bring to illuminate the path of desire we are walking.

Chapter 15

The Light of Worthiness

Where do you hope to be one day?
Who do you hope to be one day?

Beloved, we will never fully enter into the reality we desire if we don't believe we are worthy to be there. The pursuit of our deepest longings is a journey of self-worth. What we are pursuing is on a higher level of self-worth. Do you think the goal of the Giver of our lives is for us to get to the place we desire only to hate ourselves there? Only to still be trying to trade out the container we've been given to receive Love in? No! Of course not. The intention of the Giver of our existence is that throughout our lives we will continually grow into our most wholehearted and authentic selves. We must embrace our worthiness today and every day to embrace the worthiness that is found in our forthcoming selves.

I want to end this second section by offering a meditation on this worthiness conversation. At the end of the first section, I offered the practice of the telephone and the heartbeat. For this one, I invite us to meditate on what we do with our innate light.

My hope is to offer you a bit of a call and response. I will guide you in what to envision and consider. The following sentences that are italicized are meant to serve as a verbal/nonverbal response from you. Please refrain from rushing through the responses. If you sense a bit of a hesitancy in responding, that means you are hitting up against a hidden blockage that deserves your attention. My guess is it will have something to do with your identity since this a meditation about seeing our innate worthiness. Receive the grace available in this moment to receive these words as an invitation to know Love more deeply.

Let's begin.

As much as you can while you read this book, center yourself in your body.

Take a couple of deep breaths with a slow inhale and exhale.

In.

Out.

In.

Out.

As you rest in your body, express gratitude that this biological masterpiece holds your unique soul. You are an amalgamation of body and soul. Feel the gift of your unique incarnation.

Thank you for this gift of existing.

Now invite the Giver of your incarnation to join you in
this moment.

Thank you for being here.

Is there any gratitude you would like to express?

I want to express gratitude for . . .

As we invite the Giver of your existence into this
moment, let's remember that this Giver of your
existence is also the Giver of everything, the
Creator of the unfathomable everything, and let's
bring the wonder of that unfathomableness to this
moment.

You are the Giver of everything . . .

Now bring in your desire. The desire you have identified
as your bliss, calling, vocation. The deepest
desire you have for yourself, your life, your lived
experience.

When you look at this desire, your thoughts often tell
you it is an impossibility. That it's never going to
happen to someone like you.

But hold this desire. A desire that you may never have
realized was placed in you by the Giver of your
existence.

See this desire.

Hold it.

Love it.

Hold it in love.

I love you.

Imagine the Giver holding it in love as well.

I love you.

Now imagine what it must feel like when the desire has
been accomplished. What it must feel like when
you have arrived at your desired destination. Be
there in this moment. What's happening? What
does it look like? What does it sound like? What
does it feel like?

It feels like . . .

Feel it! What does it feel like to be in that moment?
What does it feel like for it to be already done?

It feels like . . .

You did it. You got there! Notice the light that is
shining bright in you in that moment. See how
it burns so brightly. It feels so good to have your
light shine so bright.

I can see the light . . .

Now come back to this moment. See the light you have
now. Find it. It's there.

I can see the light . . .

The light in that future moment is the same light you
possess now. It didn't change. You just brought it
all the way there. You are a light there because you
are already a light now. The light has
always been *here*. You just said yes to
bringing it to a desired possibility.

See your light now in the future. You allowed your
light to be placed on this level of greatness. On this
level of goodness. You said yes to being this kind of
contribution. The Giver of your light is with you in
this place.

I am a contribution.

Feel how proud you are for not taking yourself off the
path. For not giving up on yourself. Look how
abundant the Giver has been as you opened yourself
up to be the conduit to receive and give light.

I am a conduit.

You said yes to this possibility. You didn't know how
it was possible today, but the path of possibility
opened up just enough for you to see that you could
take at least one step. And then you took the next.
And the next. And the next. Your willingness to
take the next step was all the Giver needed to pour
into you all you needed to accomplish what you
were asked to do.

I am the container that Love wants to pour Itself into.

Take a moment to experience the joy of discovering
that all you needed was given to you along your
path. Grace upon grace upon grace. Your journey
may have been hard, for sure. But it was worth it.

*I have been given everything I need to
accomplish what I have been asked to do.*

Next, if you're able, look at yourself now, holding
this vision of you to come. You with your light
now . . . holding a vision of that light in your future
accomplished desire.

I am holding the light.

See yourself now. You know what you've been through
up until now. You know the journey you've been
on. You know how hard it has been for you. But
you also know that you have discovered this deep
desire inside you that keeps calling to you. You
and no one else. It's meant for you. You don't need
anyone else's permission to pursue this desire. This
light is *in* you. The authority of the light is already
in you. The authority is coming *from* you! You're the
one showing up for your life. You're the one saying
yes. You're the one who is the conduit. You're the
one who is already worthy.

The light illuminates my worthiness.

Receive this worthiness in gratitude. Receive this
authority in gratitude. It's already in you.

Thank you for my light.

Then we turn to the Giver of unfathomable possibilities
and ask, "How is this all going to happen?"

The Giver responds, "You will be given everything you
need to accomplish what you have been asked to do."

We accept our agency to say yes to our path, but we also say yes to the reality that so much of our journey is not up to us. That the Giver is working in ways we cannot possibly know or imagine. But we've been given this desire, this light, and this conduit container, and we can open ourselves up to the miraculous journey ahead of us.

I am here to receive, to allow, to say yes.

So let us finish with this simple prayer:

Dear Giver,
    Please use me.
    Please use my light.
    Please use my life.
I say yes.

The Third Argument

*it was something like this

Chapter 16

Dying Is Better Than Living

How do you think the world will end?

I come from a faith culture that believes the end of all things, the Apocalypse, the end of the world, begins when Jesus comes back to earth. Stay with me, friends! This next section is *not* about whether or not that belief is true, but I have to get very particular and personal to lead us to a commonly held conclusion. Just stick with me for a few weird paragraphs.

There's a myriad of opinions on this, but a quick twenty-first-century American Evangelical Christian synopsis is that one day, without anyone knowing it, trumpets will be heard around the universe as a golden Jesus appears in the sky, calling all his faithful followers to the clouds to meet him, while the rest of the world falls into judgmental chaos and experiences a purging and eventual cleansing of all that is evil to remake a perfect world for Jesus and his faithful followers to live on without tears in their eyes or pain in their bodies. A lot of juicy details are left out in this summary, but you get the overarching story. Faithful people get out. All the bad is dealt with. The faithful come back to a better life. A better life is waiting on the other side of the end of the world.

I will say I didn't grow up around really crazy and destructive religious people. No one was like, "It's happening! This Thursday night! Bring your Nikes." No one was that nuts. I'm actually really grateful for the kind of community I was raised in. But when I was a kid, I did notice a kind of secret conversation going on with the adults. They would say, "Of course no one knows when Jesus is coming back. It would be ridiculous to predict that! It even says in the Bible that no one will know. So, no, none of us know when this will happen"—and then they would pause, look around to see if any strangers were listening, and continue in a whisper, like the way you would tell a juicy bit of neighborhood gossip. "But we think we're at the end. And in order for the end to happen, we've got to rebuild the old Jewish temple in Jerusalem. The Muslims are there currently, so we'll need to get rid of them somehow. Hopefully make it look like an accident or something, if you know what I mean [wink].[1] And then we've got to set up the altar in the middle of the temple. And we'll need to get an unblemished heifer, place it on the altar . . . and do this and that, and then—*boom!*—the cosmic trapdoor that Jesus has been sitting on the whole time will drop from under him, and he'll have to come back and clean up all this sinful malarky."

It was a convincing story! At least, as a kid I was convinced. For one, adults told me this was true, and I had no reason to believe that the adults didn't know what they were taking about. I mean, they could drive cars and buy milkshakes whenever they wanted to. Surely they had it together. Two, I've always been a visually oriented kid, and yet I grew up in

1. In no way do I believe this sentiment. This horrible statement was something I heard an adult say in the context of the end-times when I was a kid.

156 The Third Argument: Dying Is Better Than Living

Protestantism, which has hardly any images anywhere. But on this particular subject matter, all the visuals came out! There were maps and charts and elaborately illustrated timelines! They had drawn multiheaded monsters, heavenly armies, and evil politicians who get everyone in the world to put computer chips in their foreheads. Finally! This was the story with the robust visual component I had longed for while sitting in the pews all those years. Also, they made movies about all this! I'm a little too old for the Left Behind series, but we had movies produced in the 1970s called *A Thief in the Night*, *A Distant Thunder*, and *Image of the Beast*. They were very low-budget and horribly cheesy, but I thought they were true. Why would I ever think they weren't true? We watched them in the same sanctuary where we baptized babies, celebrated graduations, held marriages, and performed funerals. You know, real human stuff. So when I watched these films under the supervision of these adults, I concluded that what I was seeing was part of real life. When I remember the nightmares from my childhood, they were not about Freddy Krueger or monsters hiding under my bed; they were from Sunday night church, where we watched all of these movies in one sitting. From my bedroom I cried out in utter fear to my mom multiple times that night.

I believed it. But then I got older and moved away from that community. I moved away from that narrative. I went to college, became an adult, got a job teaching high school art. I no longer was in these conversations. I stopped thinking about them and actually forgot that I might have even believed they were true at all. Sometime in my mid-thirties I recognized this end-of-the-world narrative had been influencing me subconsciously in really destructive ways. I found it was actually making me a worse-off human being in my thoughts and deeds. Also, as a person of faith, I realized that this narrative invited me to believe something in direct opposition to what I actually believed about being a person of faith.

End-of-the-World Narrative

This narrative did two things to me.

One, it never made me think of the world two hundred years from now, because why would I? Jesus is going to come back soon, right? What's funny to me now is how not open-minded anyone was on their timeline for when the end of the world would take place. They made it sound like it was going to happen tomorrow! Or at least within our lifetime.

No one, ever, has said, "Friends, Jesus is going to return in 3022. Don't ask me how I know; I just know. Now that's a little further away than some of us thought it would be. It's another thousand years actually, and we have a lot of obstacles in our way to making it as a species for another thousand years. We have an ever-warming climate that's starting to affect fragile ecosystems that are important to sustaining life on this planet. We have diminishing clean water supplies that are starting to put pressure on governmental politics. We have the worry of global disease pandemics that can obliterate entire industries of employment for societies. We also have an ever-increasing economic gap between the rich and the poor, which historically leads to massive bloodshed. Speaking of which, we're really good at killing one another! We have assault rifles readily available to take out as many human lives we wish at any moment. We have smart bombs and drones dropping fire from the sky. We have nuclear weapons! It's predicted that it would take only around one hundred nuclear bombs to wipe out human society as we know it, and there are fifteen thousand bombs in the world! The United States has most of them—not sure what our endgame is there, but hopefully we'll never find out. We have nonstop war, garbage islands in the ocean, children needlessly starving. There's a lot! There's a lot of obstacles that need to be dealt with for humanity to make it another thousand years, so we'll need to pull together! We'll need to work together, the whole world united, to overcome these obstacles so that humanity, one thousand years from now, can be there for Jesus' glorious return!"

No one has ever said this.

Instead, the conversation tends to imply that thinking about the world two hundred years from now is utterly ridiculous. Even if there will be all these obstacles hundreds of years from now, Jesus is going to come back and clean it all up anyway. He'll descend from the sky in a heavenly glow, announcing his return with the accompaniment of an angelic brass section. "I'MMMM BAACCCKKKK!" he'll proclaim, but definitely not plagiarizing Arnold Schwarzenegger's catchphrase from the '80s. "Oh, wow! I miss you all! I know it was a bit longer than you thought it would be, but hey! I'm back. I love you guys so much! Phew! It's good to be back! Soooo. What have you all been up to since I've been gone?"

Then Jesus will look around. "Nuclear waste, wow, yeah, that's a tough one. It's got a half-life of twenty-four thousand years, and nothing you've ever been able to build can properly store it, and it keeps leaking into your underground water systems. But hey, guess what—I can do anything! So why don't you all go up to heaven and fly around and eat all the food you want without getting fat, and I'll stay here and clean it all up for you.[2] Mop, mop, mop. I can do anything! I love you guys so much!"

And we make Jesus out to be our cosmic janitor to clean up

---

2. Again, in no way do I believe this sentiment. This horrible statement was something I heard an adult say in the context of the end-times when I was a kid.

our messes because we don't want to own the responsibility we have as image bearers on this planet.

The second thing this end-of-the-world narrative did to me was make me think I was never actually going to have to die. I mean, I might get old one day, but as I'm shuffling around using a walker, murmuring to myself, "This sucks. When do we get out of here?" I'll hear the angelic Imperial Butter trumpet sound and magically be carried up into the clouds to meet our heavenly janitor.

And look, I'm not the only one who has ever believed that the end of the world will happen in their lifetime. Check out the Wikipedia page "Predictions and Claims for the Second Coming of Christ," and you'll see that it lists all the times recorded that people have predicted when Jesus will come back.[3]

There's an interesting theme in all of these predictions of Jesus' return. Pope Sylvester II: 1000 . . . he's dead. Michael Stifel: 1533 . . . he's dead too. Joanna Southcott: 1814 . . . she's dead. Hey, John Wesley: 1836 . . . nope, he's dead too.

Do you see the theme? Everyone who has ever predicted that the world was going to end before they died has died!

The Painful Mystery of Being Here

Here's where all this is going.

With a lot of help from therapy, I started to understand that *my conversations with suicide were about trying to control a pain I felt I had no control over.*

And my ultimate control, always, is whether or not I want to be here.

---

3. "Predictions and Claims for the Second Coming of Christ," Wikipedia, https://en.wikipedia.org/wiki/Predictions_and_claims_for_the_Second_Coming_of_Christ.

And predicting when Jesus will come back is the exact same thing as trying to control a pain we feel we have no control over.

What's the pain we are trying to control?

Is it not the mystery of being *here*?

You mean I just appeared here? I didn't get asked if I wanted to appear. Did you hear about the guy in India who is suing his parents just for being born?[4] You're telling me I just appeared in a family I had no say in, and now I have to live this life, get older—whether I want to or not—and don't magically get taken up into the clouds but eventually just die and disappear, without being asked, into who knows where?

That's a painful amount of mystery and lack of control, if I'm being honest.

It's not just religion that's dealing with the pain of being here. Jeff Bezos—you know, the richest man in the world who made your last few Christmases possible—is creating reusable space launch vehicles under his company Blue Origin. He believes that human beings eventually have to leave here. "The earth is finite, and if the world economy and population is to keep expanding, space is the only way to go," says Bezos.[5]

Okay, great. I understand your argument, Jeff, about diminishing resources. We'll eventually need to go somewhere else. A question though. In the process of going somewhere else, do we change at all? The problems we have here, the problems we've created that are forcing us to leave, will a change of scenery solve them—meaning, will a change of scenery solve us? Will the move transform us at all?

---

4. See Geeta Pandey, "Indian Man to Sue Parents for Giving Birth to Him," BBC News, February 7, 2019, www.bbc.com/news/world-asia-india-47154287.
5. Quoted in *Amazon Empire: The Rise and Reign of Jeff Bezos*, PBS Frontline, www.pbs.org/wgbh/frontline/film/amazon-empire/transcript.

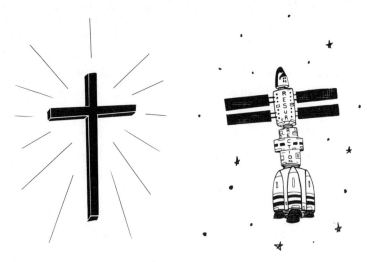

Because whether we're looking at a spaceship or a savior, what we're saying is that this dream, the dream of being here, our dream of this life, is over. It isn't working anymore. This dream has died, and we want out of it. And if our ultimate control is whether or not we want to be here, then we don't want to be here anymore.

The T-Rex of Giving Up has a very convincing argument on this one because it knows that our disappointment in life is a particularly painful, poignant, and personal death. Why live only to be so disappointed that we wished we weren't even alive? Is life really a gift when it can be so painfully disappointing? Why not get out of this failed dream, and stop living in this miserable moment, and die now? Haven't you ever surprised yourself with how enthusiastically you sang with Freddie Mercury and Queen the lyrics of "Bohemian Rhapsody": "I don't want to die. I sometimes wish I'd never been born at all"?

There can be a misery to life that makes us wish we were never alive in the first place. This is a foundational reason for suicide. Or if we look back to the spectrum of death, another way of dealing with this misery is to distract ourselves, numb out, or jump on the hedonic treadmill to forget that we are deeply disappointed in the gift of living. We don't have to end our lives completely, but we can kill off the parts of it that remind us of how disappointed we are in the way life turned out.

Resurrection Expectation

We all come to a point where we want something different. The way we've been living life isn't working anymore. We want something else. We want something new. We want the old to die and the new to come. We want a *resurrection*, if I can pull out a religious term.

But what do we expect from a resurrection?

If we were to get in a spaceship and travel across the galaxy to a new home, what will have changed in us on the trip to make us do things differently the next time?

And if we're a conscious being now and we die and we're still a conscious being on the other side of death, what will have changed about us . . .

If not the way we see everything.

We don't know what awaits us after this life. We really don't, and that is unsettling. But what we do know for sure is what happens to us right before our passing from this life, and I think what happens right before the ending of this life speaks to the resurrection we're hoping will transform us. That resurrection is found in our regrets.

Chapter 17

The Resurrection in Regret

If you were to die today, what do you think your biggest regret would be?

In 2009, a palliative care nurse named Bronnie Ware wrote a blog post titled "Regrets of the Dying," which ended up going viral globally and later became the foundation for her bestselling book *The Top Five Regrets of the Dying*.[1] She had spent almost ten years helping individuals with end-of-life care, caring for their physical and mental well-being during the last three to twelve weeks of their earthly lives. She writes of the remarkable clarity of vision that people gain at the end of their lives when confronted with their mortality. When they were questioned about any regrets they might have had or anything they would have done differently, similar themes emerged again and again.

I think you'll find Ware's observations to be invaluable and well worth a quick overview:

#5 I wish I had let myself be happier.

It seems that it often takes us until the end of our lives to become aware that happiness has always been a

---

1. Bronnie Ware, *The Top Five Regrets of the Dying: A Life Transformed by the Dearly Departing*, rev. ed. (2011; repr., New York: Hay House, 2019).

choice. Humans tend to get stuck in patterns and habits because of the comfort that comes with predictable behaviors. These safe behaviors can overflow into emotions and even physical choices as we develop an uneasiness with the newness of change, and this fear of change imprisons folks into pretending to themselves and others that they are content with their safe lives when in reality they wish they could have laughed more, spent less time being anxious about everything, and just enjoyed being alive.

#4 I wish I had stayed in touch with my friends.

Life gets busy. Jobs. Families. Moving. Schedules. And it can be hard to maintain friendships in all of life's chaos. Especially those friends who don't live near us anymore. But it seems that at the end of our lives, one of the most valued treasures we will have gained were the people we loved and with whom we lived life. As Ware says, "Everyone misses their friends when they are dying."[2]

#3 I wish I'd had the courage to express my feelings.

Ware writes that many people suppress their true feelings in order to keep peace with others, but in doing so, they settle for a mediocre existence and never become who they are truly capable of becoming.[3] These very feelings and emotions that make our lives flavorful, and taking the time to reflect on them, write them down, or even make a one-man show out of them, are what lead us to healing and wholeness. Also, Ware points out that many of the people she cared for

---

2. Bronnie Ware, "Regrets of the Dying," http://bronnieware.com/blog/regrets
-of-the-dying.
3. Ware, "Regrets of the Dying."

had developed illnesses related to the bitterness and resentment they carried throughout their lives. Then on their deathbeds, all they wanted to do was shed those bitter feelings rather than taking them to the grave.

#2 I wish I hadn't worked so hard.

Ware said that 100 percent of the men she cared for expressed this sentiment. Men find a lot of their value in career achievement and can spend a good part of their lives trying to attain a level of success that will give them the status they long for. But all the while, says Ware, they miss out on their children's youth and their partner's companionship—those important years they can never get back. It turns out that life isn't all about working. "All the men I nursed deeply regretted spending so much of their lives on the treadmill of a work existence."[4]

And pay close attention now: the number one regret that human beings express before they die and move on to whatever is next, according to Bronnie Ware, is this:

#1 I wish I'd had the courage to live a life true to myself, not the life others expected of me.

Ware writes, "This was the most common regret of all. When people realise that their life is almost over and look back clearly on it, it is easy to see how many dreams have gone unfulfilled. Most people had not honoured even a half of their dreams and had to die knowing that it was due to choices they had made, or not made.

---

4. Ware, "Regrets of the Dying."

"It is very important to try and honour at least some of your dreams along the way. From the moment that you lose your health, it is too late. Health brings a freedom very few realise, until they no longer have it."[5]

For many, something inside them wanted to say yes to these dreams but they kept saying no. Then when they were about to die, they wished they would've said yes. They wished they would have said yes to that person they knew they truly were.

Apprenticing Ourselves to That Great Disappearance

This feels like immense wisdom, and maybe you've come across this wisdom at some point in your life. It usually happens in a death-defying situation, like in a car accident or a very scary surgery—whatever happens that makes you consider your mortality and how you've been living your life. I almost drowned while surfing once. I got slammed by a big wave and was pushed deep down in the water. I didn't get a good breath before submerging and getting caught in the spin cycle of an unfolding wave until I felt like I was going to black out. Thankfully, right at the last

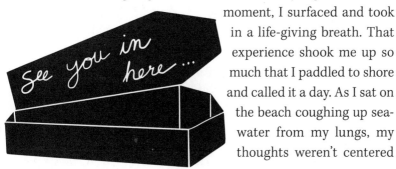

moment, I surfaced and took in a life-giving breath. That experience shook me up so much that I paddled to shore and called it a day. As I sat on the beach coughing up seawater from my lungs, my thoughts weren't centered

---

5. Ware, "Regrets of the Dying."

on how I could be smarter next time or even when I was going to go surfing next. My thoughts were more like, *I need to rethink my whole life!* Because almost drowning brought me really close to the conversation with my eventual disappearance, and it is a conversation that demands I adjust my life accordingly.

I, like you and everyone else ever, will die one day. That's the painful mystery of losing someone you love. One day they are here in the world, and the next they just aren't anymore. And the world is less bright because of that disappearance.

One day you and I will disappear from this world too. I don't have much to say about what is after this. Not now at least. I really don't know. But I can tell you from my experience that having the conversation with my eventual disappearance is one of the single most important practices I have embraced in my quest not to give up on myself.

The poet David Whyte says we must apprentice ourselves to that great disappearance,[6] meaning we must start conversing with our eventual death today and, by doing so, exhume the regrets we may already have. Regrets are defined as a sense of loss, a disappointment in some kind of action or lack of action. The reason regrets are so poignant is that they point to our deepest longings—the path of desire that has been put in us to walk, the path we stopped walking because of fear, disappointment, unworthiness, or brokenheartedness.

Or maybe you tried pursuing your dreams, and it didn't work out. It's the scariest endeavor to pursue your dreams, your desires, your deepest longings, because if you fail at your dreams, who will you be the rest of your life? I remember talking to my friend Ben about this over a little whiskey one night. We're both journeying

---

6. See David Whyte, *What to Remember When Waking: The Disciplines of Everyday Life*, unabridged audio ed., narrated by David Whyte (Louisville, CO: Sounds True, 2010).

on the middle roads of our lives, and I was talking about failed dreams and trying to pick them up again. Ben listened, and after a brief moment of silence, he said, "Man, a lot of things didn't work out the way I hoped in my life, and I guess I just stopped dreaming."

We know what that feels like, don't we? "I guess I just stopped dreaming." I just stopped paying attention to that path of desire in me. I just stopped trying. I just stopped living. "Dying is better than living," whispers the T-Rex.

Your dream died, but can I point out that if you're reading this book, you're not dead yet! Seems pretty obvious. You *have* died in some way though. Just as the spectrum of death points to, you've experienced some kind of death—the death of a dream, as the subtitle of this book says. But you're still here, and the question is, "What are you going to do on the other side of this death?" Or maybe a better question is, "What can you do now that you are on the other side of this death?"

I proposed at the beginning of the book that the Giver of our existence has been involved with our lives the whole time, even right up until now. The Giver has led us to a place where the dream could die because it was in the way of a deeper conversation.

So let's receive the gift of our death—the death of a dream—and let's get to the deeper conversation about who we are and what this death allows us to do.

Because you, beloved, are a resurrection.

Chapter 18

You're a Resurrection

Katy had worked at an architectural firm in Boston for eight years when she discovered she was pregnant. She was married, so no mystery as to how a bun got in the oven; the mystery had to do with how she was going to keep working while caring for a newborn. When she and her husband ran the math of paying for child care while still working, the numbers canceled each other out. She would make no income while having a kid in day care, so she decided to put her architectural career on pause while she focused on raising a child and running a household.

Twelve years and three beautiful kids later, she found herself longing to engage with architectural work again. It had always been her passion. All her kids were now in full-time school, and she felt a deep desire to go back to her work. But how to start again? Where to even start? She decided to dust off her drawing skills by doing an architectural drawing every day for forty days and posting it on Instagram. She viewed it as a successful experiment that made her want to take the next step of putting together her architectural portfolio so she could apply for jobs again.

Even with this renewed longing, around this time Katy suffered a massive depressive episode. She was about to turn forty (sounds familiar), and coming out of full-time parenting seemed like an impossibility. As a parent, especially as the parent whose full-time focus was on the development of her children, she felt like she had given everything to being a mom—so much so that she had ignored her own needs. She began to wonder whether she had anything to offer again. She started working with a therapist and eventually felt like she had permission to have her own life, her own work, again.

With Katy's portfolio almost complete, her biggest obstacle to rejoining the architectural world was the industry's new software, which she had never learned. So with the encouragement and help of her husband, she enrolled in a three-month program and got to a place where she felt competent with the programs. She finished her portfolio and sent it to various firms through connections she had been developing.

She got a call from a firm close to where she lived. She went for the interview, and guess what—she got the job! She was pumped, but she had humble expectations for where she would start again—most likely as a staff architect, a job typically taken by young architects right out of college. But after three months on the job, she was called into a meeting by the firm's partners and informed that she was being promoted to project manager. She was bewildered at this news. She was only three months into a job she hadn't done in twelve years. How was it possible that she was being promoted?

Many of the partners' wives were full-time household managers, and they knew what it took to manage all of those responsibilities. In answering Katy's question on why she was being promoted, they simply responded, "Because you're already doing it." A few weeks into her new job, Katy's coworkers recognized her competence in managing crises, making decisions, solving problems, and affirming others' strengths and capabilities, and they started coming to her with questions and problems. Sure, it was her education in architecture and her in-depth research into the software that prepared her to work in the architecture industry, but it was her years of experience as a mother and household manager that prepared her to be a project manager at that firm at that moment.

Sometimes we can't see the ways we are transforming. Sometimes that time we spent focusing on something else prepared us in an unforeseen way for what we would come back to. It feels great to be told you can do more than you thought you could do, and in Katy's case, her time dedicated to her loves—her children and family—translated to her other love, the work of architectural design.

But the story doesn't end there. In fact, the reason I share Katy's story has to do with what happened after she got the job.

The job, it turned out, was a lot. An unmanageable load was piled onto her as she accepted this promotion, and she was plagued with deep anxiety every day. The stress affected her eating. She would have moments throughout the day when she couldn't stop shaking, even while talking with coworkers. She would often find herself in the bathroom, crying uncontrollably. This is not a woman who doesn't know how to deal with responsibility. Katy told me that when she was a stay-at-home mom, she counted nine jobs she was doing while also being a mother. She was a volunteer for sports, church, and community organizations while also maintaining the responsibilities of overseeing a household of five. She could handle stress. But this was different.

She set up an emergency session with her therapist, who diagnosed Katy with severe adrenal burnout and recommended that she take off a month from work. She was given a month's leave of absence, and during that time she did intense therapy twice a week to find out what was happening to her. During those sessions she uncovered two things.

First, she was giving too much of herself to work. She wanted to be successful at her new job, but it left her with no time for her kids. In a way, she was running away from her kids by getting this job. She had spent twelve years doing too much kids stuff and neglecting herself. She wanted time for herself, time to carve out a life outside of her parental role. Yet as she gave herself completely to her job, she discovered that her kids actually fed her deeply. They brought a depth and joy to her life that no job could give, and she realized she needed them. She loved being a mom, with all of its complexities, and only by pushing herself to get back into architecture did she discover this truth.

The second thing she detected was that she was in a toxic work environment. She discovered that every single woman in the firm had found herself crying in the bathroom at one time or another, always after being berated by the boss. These were strong, intelligent, and capable women, mind you, and yet all of them were secretly struggling in their workplace environment. She said the CEO, although a nice man, had a military-like management style that relied mostly on shaming employees into doing better. He would shame the female employees behind closed doors, questioning whether they were good enough to do their job. He would shame the male employees publicly, in front of their coworkers, choosing to demean them as a vehicle for motivation. Katy had exerted so much effort to get to the place where she believed she had something to contribute, and yet her boss was using management tactics that constantly undermined her vision.

Katy knew she didn't want to stay in such a toxic environment, and she was the first one to leave. Consequently, the other women eventually left too. Katy took on some solo design projects for individual clients and realized she could pursue a career in architecture without it being detrimental to her family life.

"You graduate from college. You work as an architect. You're like, 'I'm an architect. That's my life. That's everything.' And then you have your family, and you think, *Oh my gosh, this is amazing.* So then it becomes a battle of 'How do I work this out?'"

Now Katy has a humble workspace at home. She has clients, and yet she can still be a mom. Her schedule is flexible enough that if one of her kids needs her, she can reschedule meetings and adapt to the life she has.

Katy says she loves it because it's a "Mike Brady" style of being an architect. Mike Brady was the fictional father in the classic television show *The Brady Bunch.* He was an architect who worked at home. Katy distinctly remembers his way of dealing with his work on the show. Every now and then, one of the kids would walk in on him, and he'd be on the phone and tell his child he couldn't talk right then, but mostly one of the kids would walk into his office and he'd stop working and ask, "What's going on, Bobby?" Or Cindy or Marcia or Peter. They had a lot of kids! The point is he was available, and his kids could see what he was doing. The work he was pursuing. His work life was integrated into all the other important parts of his life, and Katy wanted a life like that. It was only in pursuing her deepest desire that Katy was able to see what she really longed for.

The Dream That Must Die

When we're young, we develop an ideal of what a dream life will look like, and often the death of a dream means not accomplishing that ideal. But we can also keep pursuing that dream and get to it, only to find out it's not actually what we really wanted. We changed along the way, and we discovered that life is more than just working or accumulating things or visiting exotic places, but it's about becoming the kind of person who enjoys the life they're living.

What happens at the death of all we had envisioned is that *we receive a new set of eyes*. What happens on the other side of the death of a dream is that we receive a new perspective. What is the power of a resurrection if not a new way of seeing everything?

What needed to die in our dream, our envisioned future ideal, was *a life without vulnerabilities*.

Most likely when you developed a dream, you left out your vulnerabilities in that dream. You envisioned yourself starting a successful business, but you never imagined who you would have to partner with to raise the capital to make your dream a reality. You envisioned yourself running a marathon, but you never imagined you might have to work with a physical therapist to address a knee problem you've been ignoring your whole life. Or like me, you envisioned yourself on a stage performing in some way, but you never imagined the conflict you'd face in leaving your littles at home while you pursued your deepest longing.

Our lives are filled with vulnerabilities. We are vulnerable beings, and it seems that our dreams left that part out of our envisioned ideal. But the path of desire that has been put in us to walk was trailblazed by way of our vulnerabilities. Because our dream has died, we can now envision a new way that involves our vulnerabilities. In fact, these vulnerabilities may be the missing piece in our unique contribution.

Your Vulnerability as Connection

There's this moment in the Gospel texts of the Bible where the dream dies. That dream was the idea of what Jesus was going to do for everyone. In the Jewish narrative at the time, the Messiah was coming to throw out the Romans and restore the past glory of the nation of Israel. Some people thought Jesus was this Messiah. He was going to become their new national king. But then he got

 arrested and was executed by means of crucifixion. Those who bought into this future king ideal were left devastated by the death of their dream. But one morning, the tomb was found empty. And then one of the devastated community members said she had spoken to Jesus outside the tomb. And then—*poof!*—he just showed up in their midst behind locked doors. And here's what happened.

Jesus showed them his scars. His nail-marked hands and pierced side. And then he said, "Peace be with you! As the Father has sent me, I am sending you" (John 20:21).

As if to say, "I got wounded, and you will too."

Author Henri Nouwen, meditating on Jesus' wounds, writes:

> Nobody escapes being wounded. We all are wounded people, whether physically, emotionally, mentally, or spiritually. The main question is not "How can we hide our wounds?" so we don't have to be embarrassed, but "How can we put our woundedness in the service of others?" When our wounds cease to be a source of shame, and become a source of healing, we have become wounded healers.[1]

---

1. Henri J. M. Nouwen, "Wounded Healers," in *Bread for the Journey: A Daybook*

Our wounds, our vulnerabilities, the places we've taken off our armor to let others in, become the ways we connect to everything. Experiencing a death, a wound, a vulnerability connects us with everyone ever. The power in resurrection is being able to see our vulnerabilities as the avenue for connection, and it's this connection that moves us from an idealized dream to a surprising life down the path of desire.

What are you now free to do because your dream died?

It's the story of the shipwreck I wrote about earlier in the book. That the failure, the wound, the vulnerability, becomes an unforeseen way in which our purpose manifests. It's our love of our kids that makes us change the way we think our work life should look. It's our unforeseen physical or mental illness that adjusts the way we talk about what's important in life. It's the limitations in resources or finances that force us to build collaborative alliances with others who take our aspirations into unimagined avenues. It's going through the death of how we thought life would be and then receiving the gift of life waiting for us every morning as we wake up.

I remember after a performance of my show *Say Yes*, a petite, older Filipino woman came up to talk with me and said, "I want to be a speaker like you, but I'm an older Asian woman who is very small and often looked over. No one ever listens to me. How can I become a speaker if no one wants to listen to a person like me?" For a few seconds, I thought I had no answer for her. What a poignant and important question that I—a white, average-height male—could easily miss! But then I knew from my own story that her vulnerabilities were going to be the springboard for a larger connection. "Talk about that. Talk about the particularities of what it's like to be in a body that is ignored by so many, and dig

---

of Wisdom and Faith (New York: HarperCollins, 1997), July 8.

out the biases and prejudices that lead to this and what we're missing out on. I would be infinitely interested in an honest talk like this, and please invite me when you give it." Seeing her smile and embrace this challenge was one of my favorite moments ever.

I had received a similar invitation to vulnerability about a year earlier when I was still working out the details for my show. My friend and delightful singer/songwriter Rosie Thomas had seen my performance in Nashville. The next day as I drove three hours to Knoxville, I called her to get feedback on what I was doing. She loved the show and encouraged me to keep pushing into what I was doing. As we talked, I mentioned to her that one of the catalysts of crying on my toilet was my lament that I hadn't started doing this kind of work earlier in my life. That I wished I had known at eighteen that I wanted to do this kind of work and had spent years pursuing and perfecting this art form. That now in my forties, it felt good but vulnerable to be pursuing this work. "Yeah, I understand how you feel," she said. "But the truth is, you wouldn't have been able to talk about what you're talking about now at the age of eighteen. It's only by being where you're at now that you're able to bring this perspective, and it's so needed."

We must let the dream of the way things could have been die so we can get to the desire that beckons us today, with all our vulnerabilities. It's the brush with suicide that made Kevin Hines become an advocate for mental health and a nationally celebrated speaker on suicide prevention.[2] It's the nutrition inequality in Black neighborhoods that led James Beard Award–winning chef JJ Johnson[3] to invest in food education and healthy rice bowl–based products in "communities that look like me."[4] It

---

2. Visit www.kevinhinesstory.com.
3. See "About JJ Johnson: My Story," www.chefjj.co; www.fieldtripnyc.com /Our-Story.
4. Quoted in Daphne Ewing-Chow, "A Harlem-Based Chef Is Bringing a

was the feeling of something missing from her day-to-day experience that led former schoolteacher and now famous illustrator Lisa Congdon to courageously pivot careers in her mid-thirties to pursue her deepest longing of being an artist.[5]

The only thing standing in the way of resurrection eyes is the life you think you should've had. The point of our regrets is to help us see that existence has always been a gift to receive. We must let the false idealized existence rooted in comparison die so that we, with resurrected eyes, can walk with vulnerable glory into the life we are being invited into today.

We need to let this dream die so we can get to the desire that is calling our name right now.

How do we get this vision? We get it only through resurrection.

How do we practice resurrection? We practice it by going through death.

Movement of 'Conscious Eating' to the Inner City," May 30, 2020, www.forbes.com/sites/daphneewingchow/2020/05/30/a-harlem-based-chef-is-bringing-a-movement-of-conscious-eating-to-the-inner-city.
5. Visit www.lisacongdon.com.

Chapter 19

Death
Practice

Earlier we talked about the wisdom that comes from a conversation with our eventual disappearance. We saw in the regrets of the dying and in the death-defying moments that invaluable wisdom emerges and asks us to prioritize what really matters in life. So do we need to take up death-defying hobbies to exhume this wisdom? Do we need to take up skydiving or going into the woods to punch grizzly bears in the face to acquire the end-of-life wisdom that we can apply to our lives right now?

No. I mean, you can—if you have easy access to grizzly bears and a great pair of running shoes—but there are other ways to excavate this wisdom than putting your existence in harm's way. Many different religious traditions have practices and rituals to keep a conversation with death in close contact. A Buddhist meditation practice called maranasati reminds the meditator that death can strike at any time. Saint Benedict wrote in his rules for monasteries, "Keep death daily before one's eyes," as a paradoxical encouragement to help the monks and those they cared for live richer lives every day.[1] My spiritual director gave me a simple meditative practice to do on my own time that has worked

---

1. St. Benedict's Rule for Monasteries, trans. Leonard J. Doyle (Collegeville, MN: Liturgical, 1948), 16.

well for me, and I'd like to share it with you. He called it simply a "death practice."

Find a place to be quiet and alone. Lie down on the ground with your back on the floor. While in that position, imagine you're in your funeral casket. You've been laid in your casket, and you are about to move on to whatever is next after this life.

What is next? No one really knows. But for me personally I've experienced Grace *here*, and I think Grace is there too.

But before you can move on to whatever is next, you must let go of everything you've been given in this life. You need to "Marie Kondo" your whole existence.[2] Take everything in your life, find that spark of joy, give thanks for it, and *let it go*. From the biggest events to the smallest abilities, just run through everything you've been given.

I'm grateful for the way my fingers work because they let me create art, pick up pizza, pet my cat, hold my daughter's hand—and they've been great companions along the way.

I'm grateful for how I notice light in the world.

I'm grateful for the way carne asada tastes in my mouth.

I'm grateful for hearing my son sing a song in the afternoon that I introduced him to on the drive to school in the morning.

I'm grateful for that experience with the coyote in the woods.

And that midnight walk in Paris.

And that broken heart in my twenties.

And listening to Phoebe Bridgers's "Funeral" for the first time in my studio by myself, crying at my drawing table because I felt like I wasn't alone.

---

2. Visit www.konmari.com.

From the biggest to the smallest, the most publicly known details to the deepest personal secrets, as you work through all you've been given and let it go, the secret hidden path of desire that has been put in you to walk, the one you've lost sight of, will slowly rise to the surface. As you keep letting go and letting go and letting go, this path will come to the forefront. You'll see it. There it is. And you'll realize, That's what I lost sight of.

This is where you, the reader, need to set this book down and do the death practice yourself.

In the performance version of *Say Yes*, I do a theatrical death practice in front of the audience. As a melancholic creative, it's my favorite part of the show—taking us all to our own funeral. When I first put this show together, I did it in my hometown in front of all my friends, which is surprisingly nerve-racking. A couple days later, some of those friends came over for dinner, and I asked one of them what she remembered from the show. She thought about it for a moment and replied, "I remember you lying down on the ground." *Perfect*, I thought.

In some ways, that's what the whole show and a lot of this book is trying to get you to consider—the realization that you're going to die one day . . . and in that meditation, you'll become aware of the gift of being alive, and that you actually *want* to live. You actually want something from this life you've been given, and that desire has been put in you by the Giver of your existence to pursue.

But it's nothing I can convince you of. It's only something you can know by experiencing it yourself. So again . . .

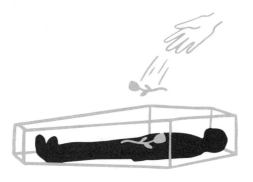

Find a quiet space by yourself.

Lie down with your back to the ground.

Pretend you're in your casket and about to move on to whatever is next.

But before you can go, you must let go of everything you've been given.

So let go.

I'll see you on the other side.

Chapter 20

Not Giving Up on Yourself

What rose to the surface when you did the death practice?
What we just practiced is a rhythm we will encounter for the rest of our lives—something dying and then being reborn. It happens every year with the changing of the seasons. In the summer, everything is abuzz with the fruits of life. In the fall, the leaves turn to brown and descend to the ground. In the winter, the trees become barren and everything looks as though all life has died. Yet with the thaw of springtime, green shoots emerge, announcing that life is returning to the world. This rebirth happens all around us, and yet somehow we can exclude ourselves from this process.

The Industrial Revolution had a huge effect on our language. We adopted a mechanical vocabulary to describe the biological and mysterious creatures we really are. We say, "I'm wired this way," as if our makeup results from circuitry and programming. We do have systems and organs, but we are not circuitry! We don't just turn off and on like a switch on a washing machine. We are biological animals, soulful sentients, who find ourselves enfolded in the great mystery of existence. We are much more complex than a machine, and part of being human is to embrace the cycle of dying and being reborn.

Only our ultimate death will lead to our ultimate resurrection, but along the journey of life, we will experience many smaller deaths that allow us smaller resurrections. The purpose of a death is to release us from a limiting way of seeing existence. *The gift of a resurrection is a new perspective.* When we say, "I'm a resurrection," we are saying we have entered into a new way of seeing, a renewed perspective, and this perspective will help us identify what we most desire. We can harness the rhythm of death and resurrection to help us stay on the path of desire we long to walk.

Whatever deep longing we found in the death practice is something we must keep coming back to, because as we move forward in pursuing our deepest desire, along the way we will be tempted to quit, to get distracted by other seemingly "good" opportunities that come our way, and we will miss the secret of a dynamic life . . . which is surrendering to Love.

Tempted to Quit

We all know how hard it is to stick with something. Just check in with any of us in February as we're about to call it quits on our New Year's resolutions. But it isn't just spending one more evening at the gym or cutting our sugar consumption that we're talking about. To pursue our deepest desire is to adjust the trajectory of our whole life, and that can be intimidating.

It can be intimidating because we'll probably feel like we're lagging far behind everyone else. Our assumption in our culture is that growth follows a linear trajectory.

We see growth as a mixture of time, practice, and learning that equals a certain amount of success. And if someone started early on in their lives, well, they have the advantage. There is some truth to this. No one is against the idea that we reach a certain kind of mastery after putting in our ten thousand hours. We all believe we can get better as we point ourselves at a goal and work toward it. It's the linear image that trips us up, because life is more like a spiral.

In the spiral model, we go through seasons of development, learning, endings, and starting anew, but starting anew doesn't mean starting from nothing. It means we're starting something new with all of our acquired life experience and wisdom inform-

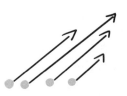   ing our new journey. You can start up your architect career again, drawing on years of experience as a stay-at-home mom. You can learn the business of real estate, leveraging the benefit of your experience as a full-time touring musician, with all the social and financial management skills it entailed. All the people I referred to earlier in this book who became successful later in their lives didn't start from zero. They brought their lived experience and wisdom into their new endeavor, which informed them as they wrote a bestselling book, designed enchanting clothing, or developed a thriving business. This is your life too. The do-overs we encounter are never a starting from scratch; they are more like rebirths—new growth from more dynamic soil.

In the death practice, I used two images—flowers thrown into the coffin of one who has died and flowers emerging from the coffin as a sign of resurrection. You may have experienced the ritual of throwing flowers onto a grave at a funeral ceremony. No one actually knows when this tradition started, and various explanations have been given for why it's practiced. One opinion is that flowers help say what we find difficult to say. They are a symbol of our gratitude, honor, grief, and well wishes to one who had such an effect on our lives. Throwing a flower on a grave is our final tribute to the gift to us that was their incarnation. Another explanation is that flowers signify the beginning of life. Placing flowers on a casket expresses a hope that the deceased will start a new life after death.

For me, the image of flowers coming out of the casket symbolizes the gift of life we can give others by practicing our own death. By apprenticing ourselves to the conversation of our eventual disappearance, we are harnessing the greatest gift we can give others—a flourishing life in which we  pursue our bliss. "I'm a resurrection" means I've listened to the wisdom that is found on my deathbed and am taking steps to live that deep-down-inside longing today. I'm pursuing my deepest longing, which is actually the best gift I can give. It's a realization of the familiar Howard Thurman quote: "Don't ask yourself what the world needs. Ask yourself what makes you come alive, and go do that, because what the world needs is people who have come alive."[1]

We must commit to coming alive. We must commit to staying alive. We do this by periodically making sure we are still walking that path of desire that has been put in us to walk. The death practice helps us keep in touch with that longing, even though we've had to let the idealized dream of how it was all going to work out die. We are walking a much more unknown path now. We know we are on our way and can be a contribution, but how all

---

1. From a private conversation with Gil Bailie as described in Gil Bailie, *Violence Unveiled: Humanity at the Crossroads* (New York: Crossroad, 1995), xv.

of this is going to manifest is a little unclear, and that's okay. We've let the dream die so we can get to the desire that's calling our name today. Who we are today—with our vulnerabilities, weaknesses, and wounds—is the way forward. But, yes, this mysterious unknown can cause us to get distracted by other opportunities.

Distracted by Other Opportunities

I'm fairly certain it's a universal rule that as soon as we passionately dedicate ourselves to a direction, seemingly "better" opportunities will come knocking on our door. Once we've decided on what we want, a very close substitute will come into our lives and offer itself as an almost perfect alternative to what we really desire. And if we take it, we'll comfort ourselves by saying, "Close enough," which is another way of saying we're almost worthy to get what we deeply desire.

There's that worthiness conversation again. Remember, worthiness is not something earned but something uncovered. It is an innate identity reflecting the belovedness given by the Giver of our existence. We have come from love, and we are meant to be conduits of love. We understand this identity more and more as we partake in choices, thoughts, and rhythms that make the light within us stronger. We lose sight of this worthiness when we partake in choices, thoughts, and rhythms that smother this internal light. We will be given many tests along our path to see if we really believe we are conduits of this light. The journey of life is about whether we strengthen or smother the light we have been given.

Let me take this from a deeply existential conversation to a practical example: I have a T-shirt idea every day. Because of this, I could easily dedicate myself to creating a T-shirt design company and probably achieve some kind of success with this idea. But at the end of my life, I don't want to have spent my time creating a T-shirt design company. How do I know this? Because when I do the death practice, that's not the deepest longing in me. I will always do creative work throughout my life. This rhythm is my deepest longing. But *what kind* of creative work I do is also in there, and I have to be wary of other "creative" jobs that want to deflect me from that vision, no matter how awesome these opportunities may be.

For example, if I get contacted about a creative endeavor I'm deeply interested in but maybe think is a bit off of what I'm trying to do in my life, I do a mini death practice—meaning I don't lie down on the ground and run through my whole life but rather simply ask myself, *If I were to die in three months, and this was the last piece of work I did, would I be frustrated with this decision?* Granted, this is a lot of pressure to put on a work project. If I really was going to die in three months, I definitely wouldn't be doing any work for someone else! So I get that. But it helps me clue in on *why* I would be frustrated. If the *why* is because I'd rather be doing something else, then I need to ask myself, *What else would I want to be working on?* And then if I can see the "what else," it leads me to ask, *Why am I ignoring that deep desire at present? Why am I not putting time into that desire right now?*

The Inner Compass

This death practice and the subsequent line of questioning help reveal a kind of inner compass we all have. The inner compass is just another metaphor for the path of desire or the pursuit of our bliss. I use *inner compass* because it's pointing me in the direction of my deepest longing when I'm being pulled to go in so many other directions by seemingly "good" opportunities. When we start on a journey, we use a compass to point us in the right direction. If we don't use a compass and veer from the path a little, it's not noticeable at the beginning. But miles and hours later, we find ourselves way off course and far from our destination.

This totally happens in our lives. We accept small alternatives and substitutions for where we really want to be headed, and years later we find ourselves feeling utterly displaced, whispering the lyrics of David Byrne of Talking Heads: "Well . . . how did I get here?" This can happen in our work, our relationships, our faith, our health—really in almost every part of life.

I think it is the pain of this displacement that leads one to find suicide as an attractive restoration option. For me, suicidal ideation was a form of trying to control a pain I felt I had no control over. Ending my life was an attractive proposition because it meant I could get out of the miserable place I found myself in. But why was I so miserable? What was the cause?

You could say I was miserable because I felt I had veered so far from a life I knew I wanted to live. *I had taken baby steps toward a divided self.* It wasn't that I hated living. I didn't hate existence. For me, what I hated was feeling like I was stuck in an existence that knew it had steered away from its deepest desires. Suicide, in a way, is an invitation to try to get back to this path of desire.

The Attraction of Suicide

One of the reasons suicide is attractive is that we start to *make a plan to change.* We start to see a way out of our situation, and we make a plan. We come up with a timeline. We problem-solve. We gather the necessary resources to execute (bad pun) our plan.

Can you see that the plans to give up on yourself are the

same steps to not giving up on yourself? Making a plan is always exciting. Seeing a way out of misery and into relief is endlessly energizing. Gathering together the tools we'll need and then taking the steps to accomplish a goal is so very satisfying. We can do all of these things without having to extinguish the light we've been given.

Giving up on yourself and not giving up on yourself function almost the same in their strategies for change. Except in the one case, we believe something new can come only through absolutely silencing our lives. And in the other case, we believe the only way to something new is through *resurrecting our lives*.

The Depth of Being

Have you ever asked what the point of this longing within is? If it's not really to attain a particular object, thing, or destination but to become *the kind of person* who can, then what's the point of going on that journey of becoming?

I submit that our ultimate longing, our ultimate becoming, the path of desire that has been put in us to walk, *is the path that leads us to God*. But since "God" is something invisible and intangible, "the name of the blanket we put over the mystery to give it shape," as Peter Holmes puts it,[2] then the only place where we can tangibly connect with that mysterious God is within the gift of our own existence. The longing is there so that we would *receive* the gift of our existence and, in receiving that gift, would step into a sacred companionship with the Giver of our existence, the Unfathomable Mystery we fathomably refer to as God.

Our longings, desires, and dreams point to a depth of living

---

2. Peter Holmes, quoted in Alexa Edwards, "Going Holmes," *Relevant*, October 12, 2017, www.relevantmagazine.com/culture/going-holmes.

we hope to be connected to. What does it mean to live out of the depth of ourselves? When we say *depth*, we mean the opposite of shallowness. We are referring to the deep core of ourselves, the place where we feel deeply and profoundly, the dwelling of our secret fears and dreams, the cave of our dark desires and passions, the underground soil in which we seek to plant hope, wholeness, and a meaningful existence. To connect to the depth of ourselves is to say yes to whatever we find there—even though it may include embarrassing inadequacies, burning hatred, uncomfortable passions, debilitating fears, existential aloneness—and receive these discoveries as the part of our beautiful humanity that is on its way to being helped, healed, transformed, and loved into something better.

That depth of life, or depth of being, is the blanket we have named God. Theologian Paul Tillich critiqued the idea that God is a being as you and I are beings. The images given to us through history are mostly of a bearded heavenly man up in the sky. Another Being separate from our being. God is not a bigger, more powerful version of us earthly beings. Tillich called God the "ground of being," meaning that the structure of being exists on the ground of God.[3] Existence cannot exist without God, because existence exists on the ground of God. God *is* the depth of being. Centuries earlier, another Paul said to a group of Greeks (quoting one of their poets), "For in him [God] we live and move and *have our being*."[4]

To pursue our cherished desire is to pursue a connection with the Depth of Being. To walk the path of desire that has been put in us to walk is to fulfill the longing that God has placed in us to

---

3. See Paul Tillich, *Systematic Theology*, vol. 1 (Chicago: University of Chicago Press, 1951), 238.
4. Acts 17:28, italics added.

connect with God. To care about our life is to connect with the Giver of life.

Why so much freaking mystery then? I remember asking the Giver of my existence why so much mystery and unknownness surrounds the path of our lives. If the Almighty really is intentional in our lives, why couldn't the Almighty just send us a heavenly fax with bullet points of the future decisions and moves we need to make to become our best flourishing selves?

A simple answer came to me in that silent moment . . .

"Because I want to keep you close."

Surrender to Love

Death will force us to experience our ultimate surrender. We will experience the truth that we are in control of very little. That we are vulnerable, finite, and powerless to do anything against the inevitable end of our biological being. But in death we also experience the ultimate surrender in having to embrace the uncertainty of what happens to us after this life. In this surrender, we discover that our greatest hope is that the Giver of our existence actually cares about us, sees us, loves us, intends good for us, and will take care of us in whatever is next.

To apprentice yourself to death now, before your eventual death, is to practice surrendering to the reality that the Giver of your life *actually* cares about the life It gave you. *To surrender means to allow Someone else to take care of you. To allow Someone else to love your life.*

If I were to receive a heavenly fax with a timeline of my life decisions charted in front of me, I would grab it as fast as I could and say, "Thanks! I got it from here." And then I'd attempt to do it all on my own. I'd probably never ask for help and probably never really talk to the Giver again.

So of course the Giver of our existence let that dream die. The dream that envisioned a future without any vulnerabilities . . . a future in which we wouldn't need anybody, especially the Giver. The death of a dream provided a chance to resurrect our perspective so we could see that connection to others, connection to existence, and especially connection to the Giver of existence come through our glorious vulnerabilities.

Connected to Love

Let me give you an image of that connection.

It's not as if when you commit to doing the work of a full-time artist, the universe takes notice and dumps buckets of cash in your lap. In my fifteen-plus years of being an artist, I've had some very profitable months and some very scarce months. A lot of scarce months actually, and after too many of them, I found myself overwhelmed by the anxiety of taking care of myself. The self-employed have no set work hours. And because it's "all up to you," you feel like you could work all day long, seven days a week. I was slowly becoming wrecked by this constant anxiety.

I spent some time being quiet and inquired of the Almighty how I should think about work. If Jesus points to the lilies of the field and the birds of the air as an illustration of how providence works,[5] what kind of image could help me find a balance between working hard and also trusting that it's not all up to me?

------

5. Matthew 6:25–34.

This is the image I received. For me, I see myself as the boat. There is a part of existence that is up to me. It's up to me to show up, work hard, and put intention and effort into what I'm doing. I must say yes to the realities of life. But there is another vulnerable part of existing that takes time to remember the context I'm living in. To remember that providence is providing in ways I don't perceive or have any insight into. That the Ground of Being (I think this is a decent illustration for such an abstract idea!) sees where I'm at, or as Jesus says, "Your Father knows what you need before you ask him."[6] I must say yes to the realities of love.

It is this provision that Providence wants us to surrender to.

It is this intentionality that Love wants us to surrender to.

It is this co-creating that the Creator wants us to surrender to.

This surrender, this trust that Someone else cares for our lives as much as we do, is incredibly hard to do. We're the ones who must live inside our lives! How can we trust that anyone else cares as much as we do about our lives? The difficulty in trusting that the Divine cares about our lives as much as we do is in the letting go of what we think the narrative of our lives is.

Building a Trust with Love

We all find ourselves in moments of our lives we label as "bad." Some occurrence that is awful, disappointing, and poignantly unpleasant. A layoff. A breakdown. A failure to launch.[7] But years later, with a different perspective, we find that our relationship with that moment has changed, and we label it as "good." For me, it was that season of obscurity that helped me find my voice. It was being unemployed that made me look to see what I truly

---

6. Matthew 6:8.
7. I'm not talking about abusive situations. That is always destructive.

wanted to do. It was my breakdown that led me to get some help and get on a journey to wholeness.

I have a friend who was in a fairly successful Seattle band that had a good run but doesn't perform any longer. He's a successful creative designer now, but every now and then, he'll sit in with other bands and play. He told me that early in his musical career, he was invited to be a part of Death Cab for Cutie and then later The Shins, both huge bands now, but he declined those invitations back then and committed to the band he helped create that doesn't play anymore. I asked him if he ever regretted turning down those offers to be in bands that became famous. He responded, "Not at all. If I would've been in either of those bands, I never would have met my wife or had my children, and they are the favorite things about my life."

I tried my hardest to *not* make a book that promises that if you follow all of these practices, you'll get what you've longed for. I don't know if you will or not! I've offered practices and pivots to help you continue on the path of desire, but I have no way of knowing when and where and how this desire will come to fruition. Also, I'm not really sure we should get everything we think we want. Have you seen the movie *Bruce Almighty* or *Wonder Woman 1984*? They are super expensive stories that explore how getting everything we think we want with our limited perspective could actually be the worst thing for us. The truth is that getting everything we think we want doesn't mean we'll find happiness. On the flip side, something "bad" happening to us doesn't mean we're on the wrong path either. We can't change what happens to us. But we can change our relationship with the meaning of that happening.

To surrender to Love is to trust that the flow of life is happening *for* us instead of *to* us. That Love is working behind the scenes in ways we can't see or even imagine. The reality is that we don't have all the information, and we certainly don't have a grasp on what God is doing. The problem is the story we tell ourselves about disappointments, about lows, about mysteries and how they fit into a narrative about whether life is for us or against us. I'm not saying there aren't hard emotions associated with those disappointments. There totally are. But what we don't know is how these low moments fit into our journey. How they form us for a larger trajectory. How God is using these "bad" moments for a later revelation of "good."

We'll have moments on our journey when we find ourselves in the paradox of being able to do something about a situation and not being able to do anything at all. We can look to this "boat in the hands" image and offer ourselves to this paradox. *What can I do today in this moment? How can I show up? What kind of person can I be in this space?* These are all ways we can be a contribution. But the other elements of this paradoxical situation—*How will it turn out? What will happen from this moment on? What will the outcome of this situation do to my reality?*—these are the ways we can practice surrendering to Love. We can move from seeing our lack of control as something that will be devastating to our dreams to allowing a larger providential perspective to help unfold our lives in a way we never saw coming. The place where we give up control is the space in which we are building a trust with Love.

We can have patience when we learn to trust that a larger Love is at work. We can't stop the waves from coming at us, but we can learn how to ride them. A wave has a low part and a high part.

In the lows, we can use the tools we've collected in those times when we've lost our perspective on everything. We can give gratitude. We can be a contribution. We can remind ourselves that we are on our way. We can remember that the story isn't over yet. And then when we hit the highs, we can enjoy the bliss of being who we are in that moment.

The American author and professor John Augustus Shedd once wrote, "A ship in harbor is safe, but that is not what ships are built for."[8]

Surrender is saying yes to the gift of being the boat . . . and saying yes to Love[9] as the ground on which that boat lives and moves and has its being.

Surrender is the practice of resting into a life that is happening *for* you instead of *to* you.

Surrender is trusting that Someone else loves your life as much as you do.

The Surprising Life

Isn't that the surprise of it all? That Someone else is intimately involved in your life already. We know this because . . .

we have an inner compass.
on the other side of dying we are gifted with new eyes to see.
at our core we have a light that shines.
we have a path of desire that has been put in us to walk.
we have the capacity to dance in the presence of existence.
we have an innate telephone to talk to Love.
we will be given everything we need to accomplish what we
    have been asked to do.
we are on our way.
we have a dream.
we are alive.
we are *here*.

---

8. John A. Shedd, *Salt from My Attic* (Portland, ME: Mosher, 1928); cited in Fred R. Shapiro, ed., *The Yale Book of Quotations* (New Haven, CT: Yale University Press, 2006), 705.
9. "God is love" (1 John 4:8).

There could have been none of this. Instead there is all of this.

The surprise is that the Giver of your life wants you to *want* a life.

The surprise is that the Giver of your life wants to love you *through* that life.

So say yes to that love.

Say yes to this life.

Say yes to you.

Say Yes.

Chapter 21

Say Yes

I wrote at the beginning that I would tell you why I was crying on my toilet. I alluded to it a little bit throughout the book, but the goal was to share just enough of my story that you could find your own story here. This book was meant to be less about me and more about you. It was meant to be a helpful guide. But now that you've gotten this far, here's why I was crying on my toilet.

My name is Scott Erickson.

And it turns out there are a lot of guys named Scott Erickson in the world. Like I can go to any wedding registry right now and type in my name and some other Scott Erickson somewhere is getting married in the next year. It's true. I do this periodically just to make sure it holds up.

Back when I started to try to claim some real estate on the internet, I found out all of it was taken. Especially because there was a famous baseball pitcher of the same name who played for the Minnesota Twins and the Baltimore Orioles (and four other teams) and was voted one of *People* magazine's "50 Most Beautiful People in the World," *and* he married a swimsuit model.[1] He is my internet archnemesis.

Many years ago, I was on tour with a band, making paintings at shows. When we were introduced onstage, everyone was

---

1. See Stephen Silverman, "*People*'s 'Most Beautiful,'" *People*, September 25, 1998, https://people.com/celebrity/peoples-most-beautiful.

associated with their part in the show. This is Neal—he plays guitar. This is Mort, the drummer. This is Scott, the painter. And the name stuck. @scottthepainter became my social media handle because I am, in fact, a trained and practicing painter.

I left my job as a teacher at a high school at twenty-seven to pursue being a full-time artist, and up until the toilet moment I'd had a thrifty yet successful run as a professional artist. I had toured the nation as a live painter at events. I had developed an artistic style I felt comfortable with. I had a number of artist in residencies, and I felt proud of what I had accomplished. I was thirty-nine at the time, the breadwinner for a family of four, and yet I had a sense something was shifting in me.

As I talked about this shift with my wife, Holly, one day, she said to me, "I know you call yourself a painter, but maybe you're a lot more than that . . . and what's holding you back is the label you've given yourself."

Her words felt like a slam into a brick wall. They completely stopped me in my tracks. I took a break. I stopped making art for a few weeks. I asked myself what I was trying to get to with all this art making. I looked back through my decade-plus career as an artist and asked myself some honest questions:

What work did I find the most life-giving?
When did I feel most alive, most energetic, in my work?
What was I trying to accomplish?
Honestly, what was the best dream scenario I could
    imagine?

When I looked back at all the work I had done, I found that what lit me up the most was not creating in a studio setting all by myself, but creating in front of a real audience. Not live painting necessarily, because my back is turned to the audience most of the time. It was when I was facing the audience that I felt the most free. The most comfortable in my own skin. That engagement excited me the most. Here I was at thirty-nine, realizing that I was more of a performing artist than a studio artist, which is weird because I don't want to do abstract work, nor do I want to get naked in front of people. At least that was what came into my mind when I thought about "performing artist." But what I was sensing was a mixture of live art creation, public storytelling, and audience participation. Some kind of weird amalgamation of all of these.

What was happening as I was putting my kids to bed, when I started sobbing and couldn't stop myself from sobbing, was that my body and soul were grieving that for the last twenty years of my life, I didn't know that this was what I really wanted to be doing. I wasn't necessarily grieving my humble accomplishments up until that point, but grieving what seemed to be a waste of time.

One of my creative heroes is a comedian who is a year younger than me. He knew at eighteen that he wanted to be a comedian, and since then he has written five one-man shows, directed three films, written a couple of books, and had a very successful career as a performer. I just feel like I've been falling down some stairs every day into my present reality. It's weird to have a hero who is younger than you are. The assumption is that our heroes should be older than us; then their lives can be a light that helps illuminate our own journey. But when your hero is behind you in years, well, it just feels like you're looking back over your shoulder at them and seeing your wasted life alongside the life you wish you had. Comparison, in the words of a onetime California governor, is a real "party pooper."[2]

---

2. In the movie *Kindergarten Cop*, detective John Kimble (played by Arnold Schwarzenegger) says, "I'm the party pooper" (Universal City, CA: Universal Pictures, 1990).

Eventually I stopped crying and had to ask myself what I was going to do with my newfound discovery of what kind of person I hoped to be in the world. With much heartfelt discernment, my answer was, "I guess I need to start pursuing this . . ."

And immediately the T-Rex of Giving Up came over to me and said, "Nobody gives a shit about an almost forty-year-old man trying to become a performing artist."

And my response was, "That's a strong argument. That's a really good point."

It is a good point, because it sounds embarrassing. Starting something new halfway through your life is a vulnerable endeavor. But I knew I needed to own this vulnerability and start where I found myself.

I had to unknow the narrative I had been telling myself about where my life was headed and had to remind myself that *I'm on my way* to something I deeply desired. I had envisioned a whole future as just a studio painter and had to put that vision in the trash basket of my identity and open myself to unforeseen possibilities.

I had to get off the path of comparison and remind myself that *I'm a contribution* where I'm at today. I started watching an insane number of comedy specials, one-man shows, interactive theater performances, and the like, and in a way I worked my way through a self-directed course on how to build a performance. I put together my thoughts, insights, illustrations, and lessons I had learned while dealing with the T-Rex of Giving Up and started to build a live show that wouldn't be boring—to me at least.

And I had to let the dream die about knowing all of this at eighteen so I could see that *I'm a resurrection* to the desire that is calling my name today. I started to present this content before the small audiences and in the venues that were interested in hearing what I had to say. I started to share on social media what I was talking about and took a risk by booking shows in places I had never been. I performed in theaters, churches, nonprofit offices, restaurant back rooms, comedy clubs, living rooms, camp cafeterias, and college rec rooms. It took me twelve times to figure out how to end the show. It took me thirty-six performances before I finally stopped changing the words. I had people who hated it. I had people who loved it. I learned so much about how to be a performing artist by putting myself in places where I needed to be a performing artist.

One night in Knoxville, Tennessee, a young woman who worked for a publisher came to a show. A year later, she reached out to me about turning my show into a book. A year and a half later, after I laboriously translated a live multimedia show into a book, this is what you're reading.

Do you understand that this is not just a book about saying yes, but an artifact of me saying yes? This book is here because I said yes. This book is me saying yes.

This is *my* Say Yes.

Practices

 I'm on my way.

I'm a contribution.

 I'm a resurrection.

Acknowledgments

Thank you to my wife, Holly, for your constant love and support. Thank you for forcing me to take writing retreats and the necessary time away to make this book happen. What a crazy year it has been to both be working on books! I know we'll look back one day and congratulate ourselves for only losing our minds for the short amount of time that we did.

Thank you to Anders, Elsa, and Jones for teaching me how to be a dad.

Thank you to my agent and friend, Joy Eggerichs Reed, for endlessly encouraging me and fighting for the vision of this book. You are my very favorite unicorn. Also a big thanks to Holly Bray and all the others at Punchline Agency for helping me seem like I'm an artist who has it together.

Thanks to Stephanie Smith for pursuing me oh so long ago in Knoxville, Tennessee, which eventually led to two books together. You saw me as a writer, and you helped me become an author. Keep up the magic that you do.

Thanks to Mick Silva, Dirk Buursma, Carly Kellerman, and the rest of the team at Zondervan who helped bring this project to fruition.

Thanks to Greg Swinehart for the "show before the show" pep talk the day after my birthday party. That story changed my life. Thanks to Justin McRoberts for insisting I don't wait until *Say Yes* is perfect before I put it out there, but use the process of performing as a way to build a piece of art. Your encouragement and friendship to me have been an invaluable part of my becoming the artist I am today.

Thanks to Jason Miller, Royal Knox, and Lindsay Bong for reading the early Zach Snyder edit of my book. I can't give you all that time back, but I hope we can remain friends.

Endless thanks and praise to Kendra Adachi for your loving, intentional editorial eye in the final stages of this book project. You helped me get through that last 4 percent, and I hope my tearful voice mail somehow conveyed how much I value your help.

Thanks, Nadia Bolz-Weber, for proving wrong the argument that you should never meet your heroes.

Thanks to Kurt Kroon for helping me not give up on myself.

Finally, a huge thank you to everyone who has participated with *Say Yes* in their spaces, venues, and hearts. This book is an artifact of a conversation I've been having over the last three years, and I wouldn't be here without your contributions.

About the Author

say yes

Photo credit: Justin Hawkins

SCOTT ERICKSON is a touring painter, performance artist, and creative curate who mixes autobiography, aesthetics, and comedic narrative to create experiences that speak to our deepest stories.

He is the coauthor of *Prayer: Forty Days of Practice* and *May It Be So*, the author of *Honest Advent*, a spiritual director to brave women and men, and a professional dishwasher for his food-blogging wife.

Scott lives in Austin, Texas, with his wife and three children.

www.scottericksonart.com

Instagram: @scottthepainter